JOURNEYS

Practice Book
Volume 2

Grade 2

HOUGHTON MIFFLIN HARCOURT
School Publishers

Credits

Illustrations: © Houghton Mifflin Harcourt Publishing Company

ISBN 10:   0-54-724914-4
ISBN 13:   978-0-54-724914-8

23 0982 17 16

4500580669

Contents

Base Words and Endings -ed, -ing

**Add -ing or -ed to each base word to make a new word.
Double the final consonant if you need to. Say the word.
Then write the number of syllables you hear.**

1. bag + ing = _baging_ __

2. help + ed = _helped_

3. swim + ing = _swiming_

4. rub + ed = _rubed_ __

5. trot + ed = _troted_ __

**Read the sentence. Underline the word that ends with -ing
or -ed. Then write the base word on the line.**

6. Maria played baseball with her pals. _play_

7. She batted last on her team. _bat_

8. She was fast at running the bases. _run_

9. Sometimes she missed the ball. _miss_

10. Maria wanted to be a good player. _want_

Naming with Pronouns

The subject of a sentence names the person or thing that does the action of the verb. A **pronoun** can take the place of this noun.

Greg is sick at home.   **Subject** Greg

He is sick at home.   **Pronoun** He

Thinking Question
Which pronoun can take the place of the noun or nouns in the subject?

 Write the pronoun that can take the place of the underlined subject. Use the words in the box to help you.

He	She	It	They

1. Lisa has an idea.

She has an idea.

2. The students make a card.

They make a card

3. Ben puts the card in the mailbox.

He puts the card in the Mailbox.

4. The card makes Greg smile.

It makes Greg smile.

5. Greg puts his card on his desk.

He puts his card on is desk

Base Words and Endings
-ed, -ing

Underline each base word. Then write each word in the
correct column.

Word Bank

fanning	flipped	dotted	dropping
wagged	pumping	jumped	planned
rented	begging	patted	melted

-ed words 1 syllable	*-ed* words 2 syllables	*-ing* words 2 syllables
1. _____	5. _____	9. _____
2. _____	6. _____	10. _____
3. _____	7. _____	11. _____
4. _____	8. _____	12. _____

Choose two words from above. Change the ending from *-ed*
to *-ing* or from *-ing* to *-ed*. Write a sentence for each word.

13. _____

_____

14. _____

_____

Story Structure

"Why is this bird asleep?" Juan asked Mr. Gilbert. He pointed to the songbird sleeping in the tree. The rest of the class turned to look. "It's the middle of the day! We should wake him up."

"Well," began Mr. Gilbert, "this songbird is on his way south. He flew all night. When he wakes up, he'll eat a lot. Then he'll fly again. After many nights, he'll reach his southern home."

"He's such a little bird," said Juan. "And it's a long trip!"

"Songbirds can make the trip," said Mr. Gilbert. "They don't need a lot of sleep, and they see very well in the dark. Let's just give this bird some space, okay?"

The class nodded and began to tiptoe away.

"Good luck, songbird!" whispered Juan. "Sweet dreams!"

Read the selection above. Then complete the Story Map by writing the important events from the story.

Characters: Mr. Gilbert, Juan, class	**Setting:** the park in the morning
Problem (conflict): Juan wants to wake up the songbird.	
Events:	
Solution: Juan understands and lets the bird rest.	

Base Words with Endings -*ed*, -*ing*

Sort the Spelling Words that end in -*ed* and -*ing*.

Words that end in -*ed*

1. clapped
2. stopped
3. batted
4. _____
5. _____
6. _____
7. _____
8. _____

Words that end in -*ing*

9. running
10. popping
11. selling
12. _____
13. _____
14. _____

Spelling Words

Basic Words
1. running
2. clapped
3. stopped
4. hopping
5. batted
6. selling
7. pinned
8. cutting
9. sitting
10. rubbed
11. missed
12. grabbed

Review Words
13. mixed
14. going

Write four Basic Words in which you double the final consonant when adding -*ed* or -*ing*.

15. _____
16. _____
17. _____
18. _____

Using Pronouns

- Use a **pronoun** to replace a noun that comes after a verb.
- Use these pronouns: *me, him, her, it, us*, and *them*.

Nouns	**Pronouns**
Bob rides a <u>bike</u>.	Bob rides **it.**
I saw <u>Bob</u> in the park.	I saw **him** in the park.
He saw <u>my friends</u>.	He saw **them.**
He talked to <u>Tanya and me</u>.	He talked to **us.**

Thinking Question
Which pronoun can take the place of the noun or nouns after the verb?

Draw a line under the pronoun in ( ) that should take the place of the underlined noun. Write the new sentence.

1. The artist talks to <u>his customers</u>. (them, me)

_____

2. A customer gives <u>Anthony</u> money. (her, him)

_____

3. The artist sells <u>a painting</u>. (it, us)

_____

4. Trisha laughs at <u>Gina and me</u>. (her, us)

_____

Focus Trait: Ideas
Details

Without Details	With Details
He looked at the people.	He looked **out the window** at the **crowd of people shouting and waving.**

A. Read these sentences about _Mr. Tanen's Tie Trouble._
   Add details to help readers see what is happening.

Without Details	With Details
1. Mr. Tanen was upset.	Mr. Tanen was upset _____ _____
2. Everyone came.	Everyone came _____ _____

B. Read each sentence. Look at the picture on pages 24–25 of
   Mr. Tanen's Tie Trouble. Add your own details to make each
   sentence more interesting. Write your new sentences.

Without Details	With Details
3. Mr. Tanen held up a tie.	
4. The dentist bought a tie.	
5. The ties were nice.	

Cumulative Review

Complete each sentence with a long *o* word from the list.

Word Bank

float	boat	blow	slow
cold	go	soaked	

1. Sam sailed his _____ on

   the pond.

2. A strong wind can _____ a

   sailboat across the lake.

3. Turtles are _____ animals.

4. The rocks did not _____ in

   the water.

5. We got _____ on a rainy day.

6. We felt _____ after playing

   outside in the snow.

7. Cars _____ when the light

   turns green.

Now use one of the long *o* words in a sentence.

8. _____

   _____

Story Structure

Read the selection below.

On Monday morning, Leah spotted Principal Hipwell in the hall. "Someone ripped the leaves off our pumpkin vines!" said Leah.

That night, Mr. Hipwell stayed late at school. He saw two young deer jump into the pumpkin patch. Mr. Hipwell explained the problem at the Parents' Meeting. Leah's father said, "I have some extra wire fencing. If I put it around the pumpkin patch, the deer will stay out."

In a few days, the leaves on the pumpkin vines were growing back. "Thanks for your detective work, Mr. Hipwell!" said Leah.

"Thank your dad," said the principal. "Now we'll all have pumpkins for fall!"

Make predictions and think of different endings to answer the questions. Complete a Story Map like the one here and write your answers on a separate sheet of paper.

1. What would happen if the deer got under the wire fencing?

2. What might the characters do with the pumpkins?

Base Words with Endings -ed, -ing

Write the base word of each Spelling Word.

1. pinned _____

2. rubbed _____

3. missed _____

4. batted _____

5. mixed _____

6. going _____

Write the Basic Word that belongs with each pair of words.

7. jogging, racing _____

8. buying, paying _____

9. took, pulled _____

10. noise, applause _____

11. scissors, knife _____

12. jumping, leaping _____

13. traffic light, street corner _____

14. chair, couch _____

Spelling Words

Basic Words

1. running
2. clapped
3. stopped
4. hopping
5. batted
6. selling
7. pinned
8. cutting
9. sitting
10. rubbed
11. missed
12. grabbed

Review Words

13. mixed
14. going

Naming Yourself Last

 Rewrite each sentence correctly.

1. I and Ann run to the playground.

_____

2. When do she and i need to be back?

_____

3. Yesterday, I and she played tag.

_____

 Underline the pronoun that can take the place of the underlined noun or nouns. Then write the new sentence.

4. The team captain picked <u>Caitlin and Eric.</u> (them, we)

_____

5. The coach helped <u>Molly.</u> (she, her)

_____

6. The tall kid hit <u>the ball.</u> (them, it)

_____

Name _____ Date _____

Lesson 16
PRACTICE BOOK

Mr. Tanen's Tie Trouble
Vocabulary Strategies:
Homographs

Homographs

Look for words in the sentence that show the meaning of the underlined word. Circle one or more clue words in each sentence. Then circle the correct meaning below the sentence.

1. I gave my mom a <u>present</u> for her birthday.

    gift   not absent

2. Does your baby brother ever <u>rest</u>?

    what is left   go to sleep

3. Are you a <u>pupil</u> in my class?

    student   part of the eye

4. Make a <u>ring</u> around your answer.

    circle   sound of a bell   jewelry for a finger

5. Please take this <u>slip</u> to the office.

    small piece of paper   slide easily

6. Please wait a <u>second</u> and I will answer your question.

    right after the first   part of a minute

Proofread for Spelling

Proofread the paragraph. Circle the eight misspelled words. Then write the correct spellings on the lines below.

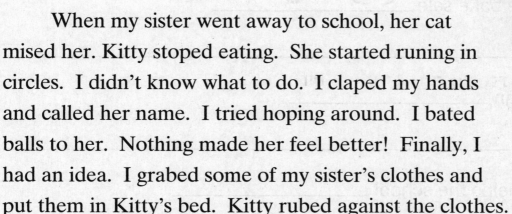

When my sister went away to school, her cat mised her. Kitty stoped eating. She started runing in circles. I didn't know what to do. I claped my hands and called her name. I tried hoping around. I bated balls to her. Nothing made her feel better! Finally, I had an idea. I grabed some of my sister's clothes and put them in Kitty's bed. Kitty rubed against the clothes. Then she curled up and started purring!

Spelling Words

Basic Words
1. running
2. clapped
3. stopped
4. hopping
5. batted
6. selling
7. pinned
8. cutting
9. sitting
10. rubbed
11. missed
12. grabbed

1. _____   5. _____

2. _____   6. _____

3. _____   7. _____

4. _____   8. _____

Put the parts of each word in order. Then write the Spelling Word correctly.

9. nedpin _____

10. lingsel _____

11. ttuingc _____

12. tingsit _____

Kinds of Sentences

Write whether the sentence is a statement, command, or question. Write the sentence correctly on the line.

1. Where is the bake sale _____

_____

2. hang this sign _____

_____

3. the money helps the school _____

_____

4. do you like cookies _____

_____

5. share with your sister. _____

_____

6. I like cookies with green icing _____

_____

Sentence Fluency

Sentences with Repeated Subjects	Better Sentences
Gustav walks to the store. <u>Gustav buys milk and eggs.</u>	Gustav walks to the store. **He** buys milk and eggs.

Sentences with Repeated Subjects	Better Sentences
Mr. Shay and Mrs. Shay need help shopping. <u>Mr. Shay and Mrs. Shay</u> cannot go to the store.	Mr. Shay and Mrs. Shay need help shopping. **They** cannot go the store.

Use a pronoun to replace the subject in the underlined sentence. Write the new sentence.

1. Gustav likes to help the Shays. <u>Gustav goes to their house each day.</u>

_____

2. Mrs. Shay likes Gustav. <u>Mrs. Shay makes lunch for Gustav.</u>

_____

3. Gustav and Grandpa go to the park. <u>Gustav and Grandpa play chess.</u>

_____

4. The store is open. <u>The store sells good food.</u>

_____

Long *i* (*i, igh, ie, y*)

Write a word from the box to complete each sentence.

Word Bank

might	pie	kind
find	night	My

1. Do you like _____ made with fruit?

2. What _____ of pie do you like best?

3. _____ mom will go to the
store to get fresh peaches.

4. I _____ go with her.

5. We will _____ the best
peaches together.

6. At _____ we will eat peach pie.

Pronouns and Verbs

- If the pronoun *he, she,* or *it* comes before a verb that tells about an action happening now, add *-s* or *-es* to the verb.

He rides the bus.   She misses the bus.

I ride a bike.   He rides a bike.

- If the pronoun *I, you, we* or *they* comes before the verb, do not add *-s* or *-es*.

They ride the bus.   **We miss** the bus.

Thinking Question
When should I add an -s to the end of a verb?

✎   **Circle the correct verb to go with the subject. Then rewrite the sentence.**

1. We (ride, rides) the bus to the game.

   We ride the bus to the game.

2. She (hand, hands) the man a ticket.

   She hands the Man a ticket.

3. You (watch, watches) the game.

   You watch the game.

4. They (look, looks) at the pitcher.

   They look at the pitcher.

5. He (catch, catches) the ball.

   He catches the ball.

Long *i* (*i*, *igh*, *ie*, *y*)

In each row, circle the words that have the long *i* sound.

1.	(by)	(light)	win	(pie)	(pick)
2.	(ply)	swim	mild	(fin)	(slight)
3.	milk	(child)	why	gift	(thigh)
4.	bright	pink	(tie)	bind	(dry)

Write a word from the box that fits each clue.

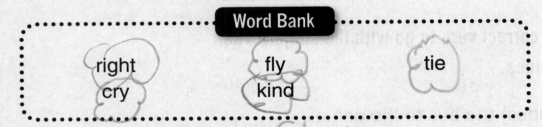

Word Bank

right   fly   tie
cry   kind

5. This is what a jet does. ___fly___

6. You do this with laces. ___tie___

7. A nice pal is this. ___kind___

8. If you don't go left, you might go this way.

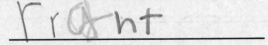
___rrght___

9. A child might do this when he or she is sad.

___cry___

Lesson 17
PRACTICE BOOK

Sequence of Events

Today the boys were playing baseball. Since Miguel didn't play baseball, he sat on the curb.

When the first batter struck out, Miguel groaned. When two more batters struck out, Miguel started whistling.

Barry frowned. "Do you think it's easy to hit a ball that's coming at you fast and hard?"

"I don't know," said Miguel. "Let me try."

"Okay," said Barry. "You're on our team and it's your turn."

Miguel held the bat. Then he saw the ball coming toward him. He took a mighty swing! A loud CRACK sounded. The ball flew up into the sky.

"Wow!" said Miguel. "Maybe I like this game!"

Read aloud the selection above. Complete the Flow Chart to show the sequence of events in Miguel's story.

Event:

Event:

Event:

Event:

Event:

Name _____ Date _____

Long *i* (*i, igh, y*)

Sort the Spelling Words. Put words with the long *i* sound spelled *i*, *igh*, and *y* under the correct baseball glove.

Spelling Words

Basic Words
1. night
2. kind
3. spy
4. child
5. light
6. find
7. right
8. high
9. wild
10. July
11. fry
12. sigh

Review Words
13. by
14. why

i

igh

y

1. _____
2. _____
3. _____
4. _____

5. _____
6. _____
7. _____
8. _____
9. _____

10. _____
11. _____
12. _____
13. _____
14. _____

Circle the letter or letters in each word that spell the long *i* sound.

More Pronouns and Verbs

If *he, she,* or *it* comes before the verb, add *-s* or *-es*. If the verb ends in *ch, tch, s,* or *x,* add *-es*.

I <u>pass</u> the rink.   He <u>passes</u> the rink.

We <u>watch</u> the skaters.   She <u>watches</u> the skaters.

They <u>mix</u> hot soup.   He <u>mixes</u> hot soup.

I <u>reach</u> for a cup.   She <u>reaches</u> for a cup.

Thinking Question
When should I add -es to the end of a verb?

 Draw a line under each correct sentence.

1. He fix the skates.

   He fixes the skates.

2. We dash around the rink.

   We dashes around the rink.

3. She teaches them a trick.

   She teach them a trick.

4. He misses a turn.

   He miss a turn.

5. He watch from the stands.

   He watches from the stands.

Focus Trait: Voice
Using Dialogue

Without Dialogue	With Dialogue
Dani wanted to go to the baseball game.	Dani begged, "Mom, please let me go to the baseball game. Please!"

A. Rewrite each sentence. Use dialogue.

Without Dialogue	With Dialogue
1. Dani asked Mom about the score.	"_____?" Dani asked Mom.
2. Mom told her it was tied.	"_____!" Mom said.

B. Rewrite each sentence. Use dialogue.

Sentence	Dialogue
3. Tad told Dani she couldn't play.	
4. Dani wanted to know why.	
5. Tad said she was too young.	

Cumulative Review

Combine a word from the box with a word below. Write the word on the line, and read the whole compound word.

Word Bank

be	box	hive
cake	boat	ball
end	light	

1. pan _____

2. sun _____

3. bee _____

4. base _____

5. may _____

6. week _____

7. sand _____

8. sail _____

Circle two compound words in each sentence. Draw a line between the two words that make up each compound word.

9. We like to look for pinecones in the sunshine.

10. She put on her raincoat and went outside.

Sequence of Events

Read the selection below.

On Saturday, Dad took Julie fishing. He rented a rowboat from a man at the dock. "Now, let's get our gear."

Dad and Julie got rods, bait, and bobbers from a shop. Soon they were out in the middle of the lake.

Before they knew it, Julie got a bite! Dad helped her bring in the fish.

"Now, we let it go," said Dad. He unhooked the fish and tossed it into the water.

"Why did you do that?" asked Julie.

"We only keep what we can eat. If we kept all the fish," began Dad.

"There wouldn't be any left to catch!" Julie laughed.

Answer the questions to infer important events. Then work with a partner to complete a Flow Chart like this one.

1. How do Dad and Julie get to the middle of the lake? Why do they go there?

_____

_____

2. What do you know Julie has done before she gets a fish to bite on her line?

_____

Long *i* (*i, igh, y*)

Write a Spelling Word for each clue.

1. This is a month of the year. _____

2. You can cook food this way. _____

3. This also means *correct*. _____

4. The opposite of *tame* _____

5. A young person _____

6. A word that asks a question _____

7. When the sky is dark _____

8. A word that can mean *next to* _____

Add and subtract letters from the words below to write Spelling Words.

9. (spray – ra) = _____

10. (bright – br) + l = _____

11. (signal – nal) + h = _____

12. (fight – ght) + nd = _____

Spelling Words
Basic Words
1. night
2. kind
3. spy
4. child
5. light
6. find
7. right
8. high
9. wild
10. July
11. fry
12. sigh
Review
13. by
14. why

Pronouns and Homophones

- Don't confuse *their*, *they're*, and *there*.

Their house is red.

They're all wearing hats.

There is my bike!

- Don't confuse *your* and *you're*.

Your house is red.

You're wearing a hat!

 Circle the correct verb to go with the subject.

1. She walks into (their, there) room.

2. (Their, They're) running in the park.

3. I can see a puddle over (they're, there).

4. (Your, You're) late for the game.

5. (Your, You're) hat stayed dry.

 Draw a line under each correct sentence.

6. Their brother runs in a race.

Their brother runs in a race.

7. Your running very quickly!

You're running very quickly!

8. There looking back at you.

They're looking back at you.

Name _____ Date _____

Lesson 17
PRACTICE BOOK

Luke Goes to Bat
Vocabulary Strategies:
Antonyms

Antonyms

Draw a line from each word on the left to its antonym on the right.

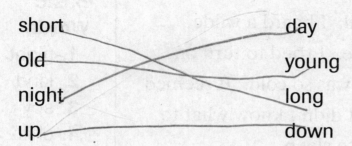

short   day

old   young

night   long

up   down

Read each sentence. Think of a word that has the opposite meaning of the underlined word and write it on the line.

1. Emily took a <u>short</u> walk around the block.

   Emily tooka long walk around the block.

2. We climbed <u>up</u> to the tree house.

   we climbed down the tree house

3. We <u>yelled</u> when the parade came down the street.

   we screa

4. A <u>young</u> cat is called a kitten.

   _____

Name _____   Date _____

Lesson 17
PRACTICE BOOK

Proofread for Spelling

Luke Goes to Bat
Spelling: Long *i*, (*i*, *igh*, *y*)

Proofread the journal entry. Circle the misspelled words. Then write the correct spellings on the lines below.

Last knight, I was so afraid. I heard a wilde scream from somewhere outside. I tried to turn on the lite, but it was up too hi. It was so cold. It seemed more like January than Jullie. I didn't know what to think. I let out a sye and went to sleep.

1. _____	4. _____
2. _____	5. _____
3. _____	6. _____

Find and circle six Spelling Words with long *i*. The words can read across or down.

Q	L	W	M	X	P	F	R	Y
F	I	N	D	G	R	T	Z	P
K	D	B	X	R	O	V	M	W
I	X	C	H	I	L	D	N	I
N	V	J	S	G	R	K	N	L
D	M	P	A	H	K	N	E	D
Q	A	M	F	T	U	V	A	R

Spelling Words
Basic Words
1. night
2. kind
3. spy
4. child
5. light
6. find
7. right
8. high
9. wild
10. July
11. fry
12. sigh

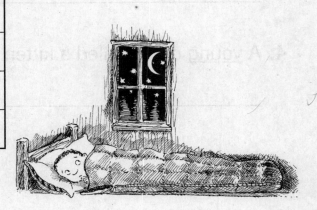

Kinds of Sentences

Read each sentence. Tell whether it is a statement, an exclamation, a command, or a question. Then write the sentence correctly on the line.

1. did you hit that ball _____

_____

2. you did a great job _____

_____

3. try that again _____

_____

4. Hanna pitches the ball _____

_____

5. her dad hits the ball _____

_____

6. how far did he hit it _____

_____

Conventions

Subject and Verb Don't Match	Subject and Verb Match
He <u>pitch</u> the ball.	**He pitches** the ball.
She <u>swing</u> the bat.	**She swings** the bat.

Proofread the paragraphs. Find five places where the pronoun and verb do not match. Write the corrected sentences on the lines below.

Mike plays baseball with me. He pitch the ball.
I hit the ball. It get dark out. Mom calls me. She yell,
"Dinner!"

I wave at Mike. He wave back. He rush home, too.

1. _____

2. _____

3. _____

4. _____

5. _____

Long *e* Sound for *y*

Circle the word that tells about each picture. Then use the words to complete the sentences below.

1.

bath   baby   brick

2.

furry   funny   find

3.

pretty   pretzel   kitty

4.

pond   penny   pony

5.

slippery   slope   sloppy

6.

penny   pencil   painted

7. We slid on the _____ sidewalk.

8. I gave my mom a _____ rose.

9. The _____ story made me smile.

10. The _____ went to sleep.

Using *am*, *is*, and *are*

The verb *be* takes different forms. *Is, are,* and *am* tell about something happening now. Make sure the form of *be* agrees with the subject.

Use **is** with one.	**The day is** starting.
Use **are** with more than one.	**The farmers are** in the fields.
Use **am** with I.	**I am** there.

Thinking Question
Does the subject tell about one or more than one, or is the subject I?

 Underline the correct sentence.

1. The sun is out.

The sun am out.

2. The corn plants is high.

The corn plants are high.

3. The workers is cutting them down.

The workers are cutting them down.

4. I is watching them.

I am watching them.

Long *e* Sound for *y*

Choose a word from the box to complete each sentence.
Write it on the line.

Word Bank

funny	tiny	lady	many
sunny	muddy	puppy	happy

1. Today is a hot, _____ day.

2. My baby sister is _____.

3. Wipe your _____ feet before
you come in.

4. Do you want to hear a _____
joke?

5. A _____ in the store helped
me find a gift for Mom.

6. How _____ children are in
our class?

7. I always feel _____ when
I sing.

8. My _____ likes to bark at
the moon.

Understanding Characters

Read the following passage.

"There," said Yen as she put the last shell on her sand castle. "It's finished." She was very proud of her castle. It had taken her a long time to build.

"Wow! I like your castle!" said Yen's little sister, Val. "Can we make it taller?" Val started to dump sand on top of Yen's castle.

"Stop!" said Yen. "You're going to break it!"

"But I want to help. I like building castles, too," said Val.

"I have an idea," said Yen. "I will dig a big hole for a pond. You can help fill the pond."

"Okay!" said Val, as she ran off to fetch water for the pond.

Think about the passage you just read. Now fill in the Column Chart to show Yen's words, actions, and thoughts.

Words	Actions	Thoughts

Yen is _____

Long *e* Spelled *y*

Write the Basic Words with double consonants in one list.
Write the words with single consonants in another list.

Spelling Words

Basic Words

1. happy
2. pretty
3. baby
4. very
5. puppy
6. funny
7. carry
8. lucky
9. only
10. sunny
11. penny
12. city

Review Words

13. tiny
14. many

Double Consonants

1. _____
2. _____
3. _____
4. _____
5. _____
6. _____
7. _____

Single Consonants

8. _____
9. _____
10. _____
11. _____
12. _____

Name _____ Date _____

Lesson 18
PRACTICE BOOK

Using *was* and *were*

The verb *be* takes different forms. *Was* and *were* tell about something that happened in the past. Make sure the form of *be* agrees with the subject.

Use **was** with one.	**The market was** busy.
Use **were** with more than one.	**Papa and Emelina were** shopping.

Thinking Question
Does the subject tell about one or more than one, or is the subject I?

 Write each sentence correctly.

1. Mama (was, were) cooking.

_____

2. The beans (was, were) boiling.

_____

3. The rice (was, were) done.

_____

4. We (was, were) hungry.

_____

Focus Trait: Word Choice Using Sense Words

Without Sense Words	With Sense Words
I took off my glove and touched the snow.	I took off my glove and touched the <u>cold</u>, <u>white</u> snow.

Read each description. Use sense words to fill in the blanks.

Without Sense Words	With Sense Words
1. I drank some juice.	I drank some juice that tasted like _____.
2. The barn was filled with pigs.	The barn was filled with _____ pigs.

Pair/Share Work with a partner to add sense words.

Without Sense Words	With Sense Words
3. I saw a field.	
4. She laughed.	
5. I ate a pickle.	

My Name Is Gabriela
Phonics: Changing *y* to *i*

Changing *y* to *i*

Read the word. Then change *y* to *i* and add *es* to make
the word mean more than one. Write the new word.

1.

pony   _____

2.

puppy   _____

3.

baby   _____

Write two sentences with the words that you wrote.

4. _____

5. _____

Understanding Characters

Read the following passage.

One morning, Mom and I were waiting for the bus. I played with the string on my bag. Then I counted cars.

"Mom," I said. "This bus stop is boring!"

"Jenny, did you forget your book again?" Mom asked.

I nodded and frowned. Then I had an idea. "They should paint comics on this bench. Then kids who forget their books can read comics."

"What a great idea, Jenny!" said Mom. "I think you should write and tell our city mayor about your idea."

Fill in a Column Chart like this one to show Jenny's words, thoughts, and actions. Then answer the questions.

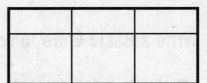

1. What is Jenny's problem in the story?

_____

2. How does Jenny solve her problem?

_____

_____

3. What kind of character is Jenny?

_____

Long *e* Spelled *y*

Write a Basic Word that has the same or almost the same meaning for each word.

Spelling Words

Basic Words

1. beautiful _____

2. dog  _____

3. hold _____

4. infant _____

5. silly _____

6. coin _____

Write a Basic Word to complete each sentence.

7. In the summer, the sky is often

_____.

8. When I smile, it is because I am

_____.

9. I think I am _____ because I often win.

10. I would like to live in a big _____.

11. Ms. Carter was _____ pleased

with our reports.

12. My little sister has _____ one front tooth.

1. happy
2. pretty
3. baby
4. very
5. puppy
6. funny
7. carry
8. lucky
9. only
10. sunny
11. penny
12. city

Review Words

13. tiny
14. many

Using *Being* Verbs

 Underline the correct sentence.

1. The rodeo is here.

   The rodeo are here.

   The rodeo am here.

2. The crowds is clapping.

   The crowds are clapping.

   The crowds am clapping.

 **Write each sentence correctly.**

3. Gabriela (was, were) a teacher.

   Gabriela was a teacher.

4. She (was, were) speaking.

   She was speaking.

5. Her students (was, were) smart.

   Her students were smart.

6. They (was, were) listening.

   they were listening

Suffixes -*y* and -*ful*

Read each sentence. Add the suffix -*y* or -*ful* to complete the underlined word.

1. The garden smells <u>flower</u> + _____ y _____.

2. I could tell by Joel's smile that he was

feeling <u>joy</u> + _____ ful _____.

3. The <u>play</u> + _____ ful _____ kitten

knocked over a vase.

Circle the word that correctly completes each sentence.

4. I can never remember to hang up my coat.

I am very _____ forgetful _____.

(**forgetful**)   **forgetly**

5. That sentence is too long.

It shouldn't be so _____ wordy _____.

wordful   (**wordy**)

6. My lemonade was _____ watery _____ after
the ice in it melted.

(**watery**)   **waterful**

Proofread for Spelling

**Proofread Tony's letter. Circle six misspelled words.
Then write each misspelled word correctly.**

Dear Grandma and Grandpa,

Last Friday, I got a new puppe. I was veray

surprised! Dad and Mom let me carey her home. She

was the onlee one I really liked. I'm going to name her

Peny. Don't you think that's a prettie name?

Love,
Tony

Spelling Words
Basic Words
1. happy
2. pretty
3. baby
4. very
5. puppy
6. funny
7. carry
8. lucky
9. only
10. sunny
11. penny
12. city

1. _____   4. _____

2. _____   5. _____

3. _____   6. _____

Write the Basic Word that answers each question.

7. I am very young. What am I? _____

8. When I feel like this, I laugh. How do I feel? _____

9. It is warm outside. How is the weather? _____

10. Where do you see big buildings? _____

Writing Quotations

 Underline the correct sentence.

1. Dad said, "It snowed."

Dad said "it snowed."

2. I asked, may I play outside?

I asked, "May I play outside?"

3. Mom said "have fun!"

Mom said, "Have fun!"

Read each paragraph. Then write each paragraph correctly. Fix five mistakes in capitalization and punctuation.

The cook said "i will make corn. He put corn in the bag.

Mama said "I will cook rice. She put rice in the bag.

_____

_____

_____

_____

Sentence Fluency

Sentences with Repeated Subjects	Sentences with Combined Subjects
The weather is rainy. The weather is cool.	The weather is rainy and cool.

Sentences with Repeated Subjects	Sentences with Combined Subjects
The students are reading. The students are learning.	The students are reading and learning.

 Combine the sentences with repeating subjects.

Write the new sentence on the line.

1. The animals are eating. The animals are sleeping.

_____

2. They were running. They were playing.

_____

3. Pedro was reading. Pedro was writing.

_____

4. The country is growing. The country is changing.

_____

5. I am chatting. I am laughing.

_____

Words with *ar*

Circle the word that completes each sentence. Then write the word on the line.

1. Dee saw a bright _____ in the sky.

    state   **star**   **sat**

2. The dog in the yard started to _____.

    bark   **dark**   **bank**

3. The children played baseball at the _____.

    part   **paint**   **park**

4. Mom put milk in her shopping _____.

    charm   **chair**   **cart**

5. The cows go into the _____ at night.

    barn   **bean**   **brain**

6. Max is a _____ boy.

    smack   **smart**   **start**

Write two sentences. Use words spelled with *ar*.

7. _____

8. _____

Commas in Dates

A **date** tells the month, the number of the day, and the year. Use a **comma (,)** between the **day** and the **year** in a date.

The pet store opened on **June 1, 2002**.

Thinking Question
Which number shows the day, and which number shows the year?

Write the date in each sentence. Put a comma in the correct place.

1. Sally got her dog on February 12 2006.

_____

2. Josh's cat was born on April 30 2008.

_____

3. Mrs. Kane bought more fish food on January 1 2008.

_____

4. Mr. Kane went on vacation on July 12 2009.

_____

5. Carrie worked in the store until August 27 2009.

_____

Name _____ Date _____

Lesson 19
PRACTICE BOOK

The Signmaker's
Assistant
Phonics: Words with *ar*

Words with *ar*

Choose a word from the box to complete each sentence.
Write it on the line.

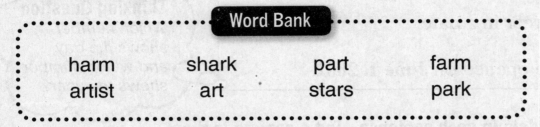

Word Bank

| harm | shark | part | farm |
| artist | art | stars | park |

1. Every Monday we have _____ class.

2. This is the _____ of the week

I like best.

3. I feel like a real _____ when I draw.

4. I painted a picture of trees in the _____.

5. Mark painted animals on a _____.

6. Darla painted many _____ in the

night sky.

Write two sentences. Use at least two words from the box.

7. _____

8. _____

Text and Graphic Features

Look at the headings and picture in the story. Use the T-Map to write what these features tell you.

Text or Graphic Feature	Purpose
Chapter 1: Rain and More Rain Chapter 2: Here Comes the Sun picture of two kids and some flowers	

Then read the story and answer the question.

Chapter 1: Rain and More Rain

Mr. Wong's class loved the bright yellow sun. But it had rained for four days in a row. The children were crabby. "We want the sun," they said.

"Rain is a good thing," Mr. Wong said. "It makes plants grow." But the children still missed the sun.

Chapter 2: Here Comes the Sun

On the fifth rainy day, Mr. Wong wanted to bring back the sun himself. The children laughed when they saw Mr. Wong's surprise.

"Now," said Mr. Wong, touching a few sunflowers, "we'll have lots of suns!"

How did the headings and picture help you as you read? _____

Name _____ Date _____

Words with *ar*

Sort the Spelling Words by the number of letters in each word.

1. _____   5. _____   12. _____

2. _____   6. _____   13. _____

3. _____   7. _____   14. _____

4. _____   8. _____

                    9. _____

                   10. _____

                   11. _____

Now, add to your lists. Add two words you know to each column.

15. _____   17. _____   19. _____

16. _____   18. _____   20. _____

Spelling Words

Basic Words
1. car
2. dark
3. arm
4. star
5. park
6. yard
7. party
8. hard
9. farm
10. start
11. part
12. spark

Review Words
13. art
14. jar

Commas with Place Names

The Signmaker's Assistant

Grammar: Commas in Dates and Places

Use a **comma (,)** between the name of a **city** or **town** and the name of a **state**.

The gas station is in **Dallas, Texas**.

Thinking Question
Which word is the name of the city or town, and which word is the name of the state?

✎ **Write the city and state named in each sentence. Put a comma in the correct place.**

1. The car breaks down after we leave Austin Texas.

_____

2. A truck tows the car to San Antonio Texas.

_____

3. A repairman calls a shop in Miami Florida.

_____

4. The shop sends car parts from Atlanta Georgia.

_____

5. Then we drive to Oakland California.

_____

Name _____ Date _____

Lesson 19
PRACTICE BOOK

The Signmaker's
Assistant
Writing: Write to Express

Focus Trait: Organization
Beginning, Middle, End

Read the story below. Think about the beginning, middle, and
end. Then write what each part tells you.

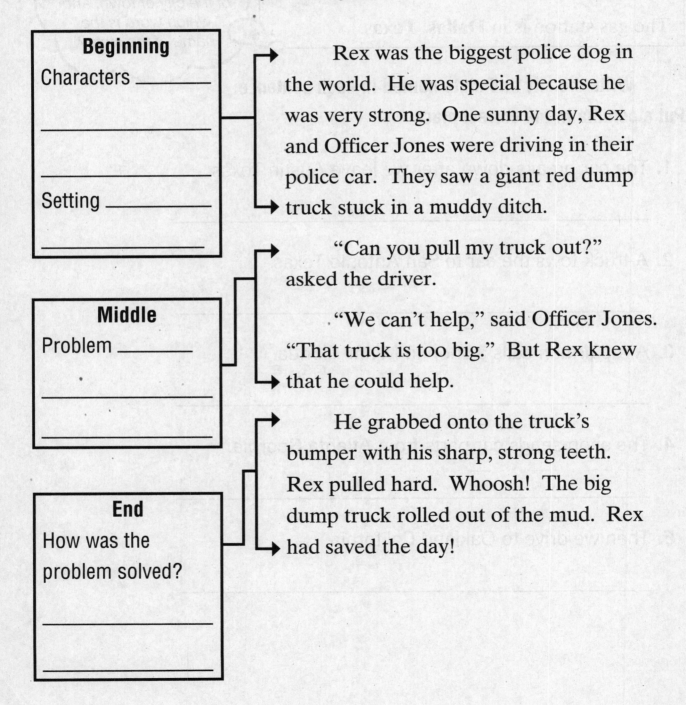

Beginning

Characters _____

_____

_____

Setting _____

_____

Middle

Problem _____

_____

_____

End

How was the
problem solved?

_____

_____

Rex was the biggest police dog in
the world. He was special because he
was very strong. One sunny day, Rex
and Officer Jones were driving in their
police car. They saw a giant red dump
truck stuck in a muddy ditch.

"Can you pull my truck out?"
asked the driver.

"We can't help," said Officer Jones.
"That truck is too big." But Rex knew
that he could help.

He grabbed onto the truck's
bumper with his sharp, strong teeth.
Rex pulled hard. Whoosh! The big
dump truck rolled out of the mud. Rex
had saved the day!

Cumulative Review

Circle the word that goes with each picture. Underline the letters that spell the long *i* or long *e* sound.

1.

light   late

2.

pie   pig

3.

shine   shy

4.

part   party

Write words you know with long *i* spelled *y*. Write words you know with long *e* spelled *y*.

Long *i*	Long *e*
_____	_____
_____	_____
_____	_____

Lesson 19
PRACTICE BOOK

The Signmaker's Assistant

Deepen Comprehension:
Text and Graphic Features

Text and Graphic Features

Read the selection below.

Chapter 1: The Stop

Grandpa and Matt went for a drive. After a while, Grandpa said, "Let's stop for lunch."

"Okay, Gr—," Matt began. Then he suddenly stopped talking.

"What is it, Matt?" asked Grandpa. Matt was just staring at the sign ahead.

Grandpa pushed down on the brake. Matt didn't speak or move.

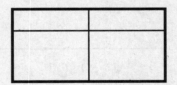

Chapter 2: The Start

Grandpa didn't see any cars, so he started driving again.

"Ah," Matt said then. He shook his head.

"Why did you get so quiet and still?" asked Grandpa.

Think about text and graphic features to answer the questions. Then complete a T-Map on a separate sheet of paper.

1. How do text and picture clues help you to understand what Matt does? _____

_____

_____

2. How will Matt answer Grandpa's question? _____

_____

_____

Words with *ar*

Write the Spelling Word that goes with each picture.

Spelling Words
Basic Words
1. car
2. dark
3. arm
4. star
5. park
6. yard
7. party
8. hard
9. farm
10. start
11. part
12. spark
Review Words
13. art
14. jar

1. _____   3. _____   5. _____

2. _____   4. _____   6. _____

Write the Spelling Word that matches each clue.

7. To begin _____

8. Where pigs and
   cows live _____

9. Not bright _____

10. The opposite of soft _____

11. Where grass grows _____

12. Not whole _____

13. A flash of light _____

14. A painting _____

Commas in Parts of Letters

Read this letter. It needs five commas. Write each comma where it belongs in this letter.

Dear Jia

    On May 2 2007, I visited Austin Texas. We had fun. I think you will like Dallas Texas, too.

                            Your friend

                            Ben

Write the city and state named in each sentence. Put a comma in the correct place.

1. The flower shop is in Portland Maine.

_____

2. Mrs. Longman calls from Los Angeles California.

_____

3. Frank Richards visits Seattle Washington.

_____

Name _____ Date _____

Lesson 19
PRACTICE BOOK

The Signmaker's Assistant
Vocabulary Strategies:
Synonyms

Synonyms

Read each sentence. Circle the letter next to the synonym of the underlined word.

1. This room has a <u>large</u> door and a small window.

   a. big   **b. tiny**

2. The light is too <u>dim</u>. It doesn't help me see.

   a. high   **b. dark**

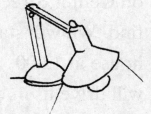

3. Tom wanted a <u>tall</u> ladder. He needed to reach the top shelf.

   a. low   **b. high**

4. The flowers grew <u>below</u> the bushes. They were hard to see.

   a. under   **b. beside**

5. The kitten was <u>frail</u>. He couldn't run at all.

   a. strong   **b. weak**

6. We wanted to <u>toss</u> an apple, but Mom said to use a ball.

   a. throw   **b. eat**

Proofread for Spelling

Proofread the invitation. Circle the six misspelled words. Then write the correct spellings on the lines below.

Dear Kara,

You are invited to my paurty.

It will be in the parke
on Center Street. It is not heard to
find. We will starrt from my
house at 12:00. My mother
will drive us in her kar.
We will be home before dirk.

Your friend,
Angie

Spelling Words

**Basic
Words**
1. car
2. dark
3. arm
4. star
5. park
6. yard
7. party
8. hard
9. farm
10. start
11. part
12. spark

1. _____   4. _____

2. _____   5. _____

3. _____   6. _____

Write these other Spelling Words in ABC order: *part, star, yard, farm, arm, spark.*

7. _____   10. _____

8. _____   11. _____

9. _____   12. _____

Writing Proper Nouns

 Write the name of each underlined word correctly.

1. The store is closed on <u>thursday</u>.

_____

2. That day is <u>thanksgiving</u>.

_____

3. They put up a sign early in <u>november</u>.

_____

 Read the paragraph. Write words from the box to tell when.

My mom loves _____.

The holiday is _____. She wants

flowers. Dad buys them at Lou's Flower Shop.

Mom's birthday is in _____.

Dad loves _____. He wants

to sleep late. Mom says he gets to sleep late

_____!

Word Box

July
every Saturday
next Sunday
Mother's Day
Father's Day

Conventions

Not Correct	Correct
The sports shop opened on May 8 1998.	The sports shop opened on <u>May 8</u>, <u>1998</u>.

Not Correct	Correct
The soccer ball was made in Detroit Michigan.	The soccer ball was made in <u>Detroit</u>, <u>Michigan</u>.

Proofread the sentences for missing commas. Rewrite each sentence correctly.

1. The store opened on March 15 1999.

_____

2. It is in Charleston South Carolina.

_____

3. Mr. Thomas sold ice skates on December 1 2000.

_____

4. He sold beach balls on June 5 2001.

_____

5. He sold shells from Daytona Beach Florida.

_____

Lesson 20
PRACTICE BOOK

Words with *or*, *ore*

Dex: The Heart of a Hero
Phonics: Words with *or*, *ore*

Write words to complete the sentences. Use words from the box.

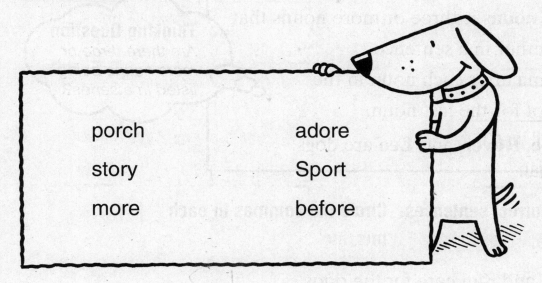

porch	adore
story	Sport
more	before

1. This is a _____ about my dog.

2. His name is _____.

3. He sleeps on the _____.

4. We play _____ I go to school.

5. After school, we play some _____.

6. I _____ my dog!

Name _____ Date _____

Commas in a Series of Nouns

- A **series of nouns** is three or more nouns that appear together in a sentence.
- Use a comma after each noun in the series except for the last noun.

Sparky, **Spike**, **Rover**, and **Leo** are dogs.

Thinking Question
Are there three or more nouns being listed in a series?

Find the correct sentences. Circle the commas in each correct sentence.

1. Mom Dad, and Kim care for the dogs.
   Mom, Dad, and Kim care for the dogs.
   Mom, Dad, and, Kim, care for the dogs.

2. Dogs, cats, and birds are great pets.
   Dogs cats and birds are great pets.
   Dogs, cats, and, birds are great pets.

3. Max, Harry, and, Grace are puppies.
   Max, Harry, and Grace are puppies.
   Max, Harry, and Grace, are puppies.

4. Puppies need food, water, and, love.
   Puppies need food water and, love.
   Puppies need food, water, and love.

Words with *or, ore*

Write a word from the box to answer each riddle.

Word Bank

~~wore~~
~~short~~
chore
corn
~~snore~~
stork

1. a sound made when sleeping _____snore_____

2. a farm plant _____corn_____

3. a kind of bird _____stork_____

4. not tall _____short_____

5. put on a coat _____wore_____

6. a small job _____chore_____

Write two sentences. Use two words from the box.

7. _____I like corn, so good._____

8. _____My Dad snores at night._____

Compare and Contrast

Sam the Rattlesnake liked being scary. But the other animals didn't like being scared. Whenever they heard the "shake, shake, shake" of his tail, they ran to hide.

After a while, Sam got tired of being alone. He decided to be friendly for a change.

That very day, Sam saw Rabbit trying to pull up a carrot. Sam pulled up the carrot with his tail and gave it to Rabbit.

"Thanks, Sam!" said Rabbit.

Then Sam saw Squirrel trying to grab an acorn. Sam grabbed the acorn with his fangs and gave it to Squirrel.

"Thanks, Sam!" said Squirrel.

Soon the animals stopped being scared of Sam. They started listening for the "shake, shake, shake" of Sam's tail. That sound told them that help was on the way!

Read the story above. Then complete the Venn Diagram to show how Sam changed.

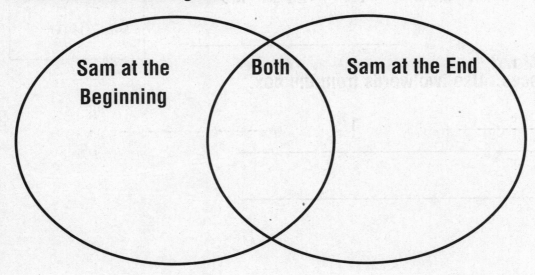

Words with *or*, *ore*

Sort the Basic Words.

or Words	*ore* Words
1. _____	9. _____
2. _____	10. _____
3. _____	11. _____
4. _____	12. _____
5. _____	
6. _____	
7. _____	
8. _____	

Write one more *or* word you know. Then write one more *ore* word.

or Word	*ore* Word
13. _____	14. _____

Spelling Words

Basic Words
1. horn
2. story
3. fork
4. score
5. store
6. corn
7. morning
8. shore
9. short
10. born
11. tore
12. forget

Review Words
13. for
14. more

Commas in a Series of Verbs

- A **series of verbs** is three or more verbs that appear together in a sentence.
- Use a comma after each verb in a series except the last verb.

Hamster **runs**, **leaps**, and **waves**.

Thinking Question
Are there three or more verbs listed in a series?

Look at the underlined verbs in each sentence. Write each sentence correctly. Put commas in the correct places.

1. Chipmunk <u>slips falls and cries</u>.

_____

2. Hamster <u>dashes jumps and helps</u>.

_____

3. Chipmunk <u>smiles skips and dances</u>.

_____

4. The animals <u>wave cheer and shout</u>.

_____

5. Hamster <u>laughs bows and leaves</u>.

_____

Focus Trait: Organization
Interesting Beginnings

Dex: The Heart of a Hero
Writing: Write to Express

Uninteresting Beginning	Interesting Beginning
Once there was a cat named Freddy.	Freddy was a fluffy black cat. He was so smart that he could solve mysteries for his friends.

Write two different beginnings for a story about a deep-sea diving dog. Make each beginning interesting. Check the one you like better.

1. _____

    _____

    _____

    _____

2. _____

    _____

    _____

    _____

Cumulative Review

Read the clue. Circle the word that matches.

1. A dog will do this.   store   (bark)   shark

2. It means **begin**.   (start)   dart   north

3. It is part of the body.   farm   more   (arm)

4. You play here.   star   (park)   pork

5. It means **big**.   (large)   porch   spark

6. You ride in this.   art   (car)   born

Compare and Contrast

Boo the Cat always hid under a bush. She wanted to be brave and sit in the sun. But Boo was scared of everything, including her own name — Boo! So Boo kept hiding.

One day, some nice kittens sat near Boo. Then Boo saw Broozer, the meanest dog in the neighborhood, sneaking up behind the kittens. Boo was afraid of Broozer, but she couldn't let him bother those kittens.

Boo ran up to Broozer and looked him in the eye. She felt her bravery grow inside her. Boo let out a loud screech — and Broozer ran away!

After that, Boo the Brave spent every day in the sun, talking and laughing with her kitten friends.

Answer the questions below. Then use a Venn diagram to show how you and Boo are the same and different.

1. Think about something you have done to help someone. What was the same about what you did in your life and what Boo does to help the kittens? _Prutect my baby brother._

2. What was different about what you did and what Boo does? _I didtoke my brother some were tus._

Words with *or*, *ore*

Write a Basic Word for each meaning.

1. A place where you buy things _____ s+ore

2. The opposite of *tall* _____ short

3. Early hours of the day _____

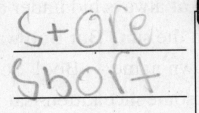

4. A food _____ corn

5. Something you blow _____ horn

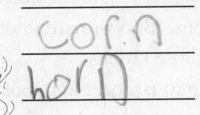

6. Land near water _____

Complete each sentence with a Basic Word.

7. Do not _____ your homework!

8. I was _____ on the 4th of July.

9. Please read me a _____.

10. I always use a _____ to eat.

11. Alan _____ his jacket when

    he fell.

12. We won by a _____

    of 3 to 2.

Spelling Words
Basic Words
1. horn
2. story
3. fork
4. score
5. store
6. corn
7. morning
8. shore
9. short
10. born
11. tore
12. forget
Review Words
13. for
14. more

Commas in a Series

 Draw a line under each correct sentence.

1. Super Cat visits the park, school, and, playground.

Super Cat visits the park, school, and playground.

Super Cat, visits the, park, school and playground.

2. She saves a butterfly, worm, and ladybug.

She saves a, butterfly, worm, and ladybug.

She saves a butterfly, worm and ladybug.

3. Mama Papa, and Baby Cat, are happy!

Mama, Papa and Baby, Cat are happy!

Mama, Papa, and Baby Cat are happy!

 Write each sentence. Use commas correctly.

4. The penguins waddle jump and slide.

the Penguins waddle Juraddle

5. They dive splash and swim.

they dive, Splash, swimme

6. People watch point and smile.

PeoPle watch point, smm

Lesson 20
PRACTICE BOOK

Prefix *over-*

Dex: The Heart of a Hero
Vocabulary Strategies:
Prefix *over-*

Read each sentence. Fill in the blank with one of the words in the box.

> ### Word Box
>
> overlooked   overcrowded   overboard
> overeat   overdue   overflowed

1. I don't want to _____ at
   dinner. I want to save room for dessert!

2. Too many people came to the party, so the room

   was _____.

3. Tom can't find his book on the shelf. Maybe he

   _____ it.

4. I poured too much milk in my cup, and it

   _____.

5. The movies we rented are _____.

   We should have returned them last week.

6. I went on a boat ride last week, and my sunglasses

   fell _____!

Proofread for Spelling

**Proofread the ad. Cross out the five misspelled words.
Then write the correct spellings in the margin.**

Come to our grocery stour!

Big sale on korn!

The sale begins at 8:00 in the mourning.

Sale items are in shart supply.

They won't last long!

Don't furget!

Spelling Words
Basic Words
1. horn
2. story
3. fork
4. score
5. store
6. corn
7. morning
8. shore
9. short
10. born
11. tore
12. forget

**Unscramble the letters to spell a Basic Word.
Write the word on the line.**

1. rnbo _____

2. orkf _____

3. soreh _____

4. hnor _____

5. erot _____

6. styor _____

7. crose _____

Writing Book Titles

✏️ **Rewrite each sentence. Write the book titles correctly. Use capital letters when needed.**

1. My favorite book is the cat in the hat.

_____

2. Did Dr. Rames write the book taking care of pets?

_____

✏️ **Fix the mistakes in the paragraph. Write the paragraph correctly.**

    Mr. Grady owns a book store. Today, Lynn buys the book caring for dogs. Mr. Grady also sells her another book. This one is called how to keep a bird.

_____

_____

_____

_____

Sentence Fluency

Short, Choppy Sentences	Smoother Sentence with Commas
Sam ate dinner. Izzy ate dinner. Mario ate dinner.	Sam, Izzy, and Mario ate dinner.

Short, Choppy Sentences	Smoother Sentence with Commas
The monkeys had bananas. The monkeys had apples. The monkeys had carrots.	The monkeys had bananas, apples, and carrots.

Read each group of sentences. Combine the three sentences. Use commas correctly.

1. The monkeys climbed trees.

   The monkeys climbed vines.

   The monkeys climbed ropes.

   _____

2. Owl watched the monkeys.

   Ant watched the monkeys.

   Tiger watched the monkeys.

   _____

3. The monkeys jumped on the rocks.

   The monkeys climbed on the rocks.

   The monkeys ate on the rocks.

   _____

Words with *er*

Circle the word that fits in each sentence.
Underline the letters that stand for the *er* sound.
Then write the word to complete the sentence.

1. store   tree   corner

The bank is on the _____.

2. water   hose   watch

The plants need _____.

3. pencil   notebook   paper

Get your pen and a sheet of _____.

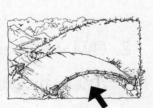

4. road   river   hill

We can catch fish in the _____.

5. head   herd   horses

A group of horses is called a _____.

How Things Look

An **adjective** is a word that tells how something looks.

Adjectives can tell size, color, shape, or how many.

Penguins look **short**.

Thinking Question
Which word tells more about how something looks?

Write the adjective from the box that best fits each sentence. Use the clues in ().

round	small	four	black

1. I see _____ penguins on the ice.
(tell how many)

2. The penguins stand in a _____ circle.
(tell shape)

3. They are _____ and white. (tell color)

4. The baby penguin is _____. (tell size)

Words with *er*

Put the letters together to write a word with *er*.

1. f + a + t + h + er = _____

2. c + o + m + p + u + t + er = _____

3. w + h + i + s + k + er + s = _____

4. t + o + a + s + t + er = _____

5. b + a + k + er = _____

**Now use the *er* words you wrote to complete the
sentences below.**

6. I put my bread in the _____.

7. My cat has long _____ on her face.

8. The _____ sells cookies and pies.

9. I eat dinner with my mother and _____.

10. I play games on the _____.

Name _____ Date _____

Lesson 21
PRACTICE BOOK

Penguin Chick
Introduce Comprehension:
Main Ideas and Details

Main Ideas and Details

Antarctica is a very cold, dry, and windy place. Most of Antarctica is covered by ice. The ice is one mile thick!

Only a few animals live in Antarctica. These animals have fat on their bodies, called "blubber," which keeps them warm. People don't have blubber. Even special clothes aren't enough to keep a person safe from the cold in Antarctica. When scientists go to Antarctica to study the weather, they must be careful. Their skin can freeze in 30 seconds there.

There isn't enough water for lots of plants in Antarctica. Only tiny plants grow there for a few weeks in the summer.

Antarctica is a difficult place to live.

Read the selection above. Then complete the Idea-Support Map below to show the main idea and supporting details.

Words with *er*

Sort the Spelling Words.

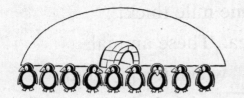 

Words that end in *er*	**Words with *er* in middle**
1. _____	11. _____
2. _____	12. _____
3. _____	13. _____
4. _____	14. _____
5. _____	
6. _____	
7. _____	
8. _____	
9. _____	
10. _____	

Spelling Words

Basic Words
1. father
2. over
3. under
4. herd
5. water
6. verb
7. paper
8. cracker
9. offer
10. cover
11. germ
12. master

Review Words
13. fern
14. ever

Underline the letter or letters that make the *er* sound in each word.

How Things Taste and Smell

Adjectives can tell how something tastes.

Adjectives can also tell how something smells.

The ocean smells **fishy**.

The water tastes **salty**.

Thinking Question
Which word tells more about how something tastes or smells?

Find the adjective in each sentence. The adjective tells more about the underlined word. Write the adjective.

1. The penguins eat the tasty <u>fish</u>.

_____

2. They drink the salty <u>water</u>.

_____

3. The penguins like smelly <u>seafood</u>.

_____

4. The <u>air</u> smells fresh.

_____

5. They love the taste of sweet <u>squid</u>.

_____

Focus Trait: Word Choice
Using Exact Words

Without Exact Words	With Exact Words
In Antarctica there is <u>nothing</u> to build a nest with.	In Antarctica there are **no twigs, leaves, grass, or mud** to build a nest with.

A. Read each sentence. Replace each underlined word with more exact words.

Without Exact Words	With Exact Words
1. The egg stays <u>comfortable</u> in the brood patch.	The egg stays _____ in the brood patch.
2. The penguin fathers <u>are</u> together in a group.	The penguin fathers _____ together in a group.

B. Pair/Share Work with a partner to brainstorm exact words to replace the underlined words in the sentence.

Without Exact Words	With Exact Words
3. With his <u>mouth</u>, the penguin father <u>puts</u> the egg onto his feet.	
4. After the chick <u>comes out of the egg</u>, its wet feathers dry and become fluffy and gray.	

Words with *ir, ur*

1. Write **X** on the bigger **bird**.
Write **bird**.

_____

2. Draw stripes on the **shirt**.
Write **shirt**.

_____

3. Color the one we can **burn** to
make light. Write **burn**.

_____

4. Circle the **birthday** cake.
Write **birthday**.

_____

5. Write **X** on **Thursday**.
Write **Thursday**.

_____

October

Monday	Tuesday	Wednesday	Thursday	Friday
		1	2	3

Main Ideas and Details

It used to be impossible to get to Antarctica's South Pole. There were miles of ice to walk across. There was no food along the way. The temperatures were 120 degrees below zero. There were no buildings or people.

Finally, in 1911, Roald Amundsen and five other men made it to the South Pole. They used sled dogs to pull them. They ate seal meat for food. They had clothes that were warm enough.

Today, many people have visited Antarctica. But they still need to wear the right clothes. They still need to eat the right food. Getting to the South Pole is still difficult.

Read the selection above. Answer the questions about the main idea and details. Complete an Idea-Support Map like the one here.

1. What was a trip to the South Pole like a long time ago? Which details support this idea? _____

   _____

   _____

   _____

2. What is a trip to the South Pole like today? Which details support this idea? _____

   _____

   _____

Words with *er*

Write the Spelling Word that means almost the same as each word.

1. blanket _____
2. above _____
3. share _____

4. below _____
5. group _____
6. dad _____

Write the Spelling Word that rhymes with each word.

7. worm _____
8. turn _____
9. daughter _____

10. curb _____
11. clever _____
12. plaster _____

Spelling Words

Basic Words
1. father
2. over
3. under
4. herd
5. water
6. verb
7. paper
8. cracker
9. offer
10. cover
11. germ
12. master

Review Words
13. fern
14. ever

How Things Feel and Sound

Write the adjective from the box that best fits each sentence.

howling	loud	icy	slippery

1. Penguins stand in the _____ wind. (sound)

2. The father penguin has a _____ voice. (sound)

3. Penguins swim in _____ oceans. (feel)

4. They catch _____ fish with their beaks. (feel)

Find the adjective in each sentence. Write the word that tells more about the underlined word.

5. The penguins hear splashing <u>water</u>.

_____

6. They step on the pointy <u>rocks</u>.

_____

7. Penguin chicks have fluffy <u>feathers</u>.

_____

8. The penguins make whistling <u>sounds</u>.

_____

Name _____ Date _____

Lesson 21
PRACTICE BOOK

Penguin Chick
Vocabulary Strategies:
Dictionary Entry

Dictionary Entry

**Read each sentence. Use the dictionary entries to help
you decide what the word means. Write the definition
on the line.**

creature	**1.** an animal
	2. a strange or imaginary living thing
shuffle	**1.** to walk without picking up your feet
	2. to mix cards or papers so they are in a different order
swallow	**1.** to make food or drink go down your throat
	2. a small bird with pointed wings and a tail with two points
webbed	**1.** having skin that connects the toes or fingers
	2. made of something that looks or feels like a web: *My purse has a webbed strap.*

1. Kim had to <u>swallow</u> her food before she could talk.

_____

2. I will <u>shuffle</u> the cards before we start the game.

_____

3. We saw a silly blue <u>creature</u> on TV.

_____

4. Frogs have <u>webbed</u> feet to help them swim and hop.

_____

Proofread for Spelling

Circle the misspelled words in the items below. Then write the correct spellings on the lines.

Make a Good Snack

1. Wash your hands with soap and wotter. You do not want to get a jerm on your snack.

_____   _____

2. Cuver a craker with peanut butter. Place another one on top.

_____   _____

3. Put a payper napkin undr your snack. Pour a glass of milk.

_____   _____

4. You are now the mayster of snacks! Why not ofer one to your mother or fathr?

_____   _____   _____

Spelling Words
Basic Words
1. father
2. over
3. under
4. herd
5. water
6. verb
7. paper
8. cracker
9. offer
10. cover
11. germ
12. master

Unscramble the letters to spell a Basic Word.

5. berv _____   **7.** dher _____

6. ervo _____

Subject Pronouns

Circle the correct subject pronouns to replace the underlined nouns.

1. <u>The snow</u> is deep. (She, It)

2. <u>Deshan</u> and <u>Ben</u> watch the penguins. (He, They)

3. <u>Ben</u> takes a picture. (She, He)

Read the sentences. Find the repeated subjects. Use a subject pronoun in place of each underlined subject. Write the new sentences.

4. Ms. Towers has a film about penguins. <u>Ms. Towers</u> shows the film to her class.

_____

_____

5. The penguins slide over the ice. <u>The penguins</u> use their flippers to push forward.

_____

_____

6. Maria likes the film. <u>Maria</u> wants to see it again.

_____

_____

Sentence Fluency

Short, Choppy Sentences	Longer, Smooth Sentence
The penguins were hungry. The penguins were tired.	The penguins were hungry and tired.

✏️ **Read each pair of sentences. Join the sentences using**
and between the two adjectives. Write the new sentence.

1. The penguin was cold.

The penguin was wet.

_____

2. The rain was heavy.

The rain was pounding.

_____

3. The egg was warm.

The egg was covered.

_____

4. The sky was cloudy.

The sky was dark.

_____

Homophones

Read the two homophones in each box. Then choose the word that goes on each line. Read the completed sentences.

1. I _____ my bike on

a bumpy _____.

rode
road

2. Let's _____ at the

store to buy _____.

meat
meet

3. Sam read a _____ about

a dog wagging its _____.

tale
tail

4. I can _____ the waves of the

_____ crashing on the shore.

sea
see

5. Jason is _____ from

being sick all _____.

weak
week

Using *a, an,* and *the*

- The words *a* and *an* are special adjectives.
  They are used before nouns that name one.
- Use *a* before a noun that
  begins with a **consonant sound**.
  Use *an* before a noun that begins with
  a **vowel sound**.

  Gabby is **a** friend. She eats **an** apple.

The word *the* is also a special adjective.

It points out a specific noun or pronoun.

You can use it with one or more than one.

The painting on stage is beautiful.

> **Thinking Question**
> *Does the noun after it start with a consonant sound or a vowel sound?*

✏️ **Draw a line under the word in ( ) that correctly completes each sentence. Write the sentence.**

1. I give Gabby (a, an) sandwich.

I give gabby a sandwich

2. She adds (a, an) onion to it.

She adds onion to it

3. Gabby buys (the, an) pear.

Galby buys the Pear.

4. I feel (a, an) raindrop.

I feel a raindrop.

Homophones

Choose a word from the box to complete each sentence.

Write the word on the line. Read each completed sentence.

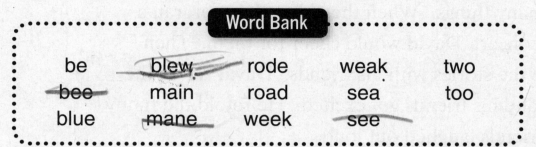

Word Bank

be	blew	rode	weak	two
bee	main	road	sea	too
blue	mane	week	see	

1. The wind _____blew_____ the door open.

2. Please save _____mane_____ seats at lunch.

3. This flower has a _____bee_____ on it!

4. Tim _____s rode_____ his dad's bike.

5. There are seven days in one _____.

6. I like to swim in the salty _____.

7. What is the _____ idea on that page?

8. There is _____ much noise.

9. My favorite color is _____.

10. It is too dark to _____.

Understanding Characters

David wasn't sure what he was good at. But his brothers were good at many things. When they played soccer, ran a race, or had a concert, David would cheer for them. Then he would share the stories with his friends. David retold the exciting parts, and his friends got excited. He retold the funny parts, and his friends laughed out loud.

"Your stories are great, David," said his best friend Peter. "You should write them down."

So David wrote about the time his brothers won the soccer cup. He wrote about the time his brother sat on the guitar. Soon, David's stories were famous.

"I know what my brothers are good at," said David. "And I know what I'm good at, too!"

Read the story above. Complete the Column Chart to show David's words, actions, and thoughts.

Words	Actions	Thoughts
faous, share funny. frends. laugh.	he writes story leters stories or mares hes frends lauth	at first hes not so he watches good at. time en he knows wate he is good

Homophones

Sort the Spelling Words. Write the Spelling Word that sounds the same as the given word.

1. sea _____

2. bee _____

3. week _____

4. two _____

5. meet _____

6. tail _____

7. mane _____

Now sort the Spelling Words by vowel sounds. The first one is done for you.

Long *e*	Long *a*	*oo* sound
sea		
_____	_____	_____
_____	_____	
_____	_____	
_____		
_____		
_____		

Spelling Words

Basic Words
1. meet
2. meat
3. week
4. weak
5. mane
6. main
7. tail
8. tale
9. be
10. bee
11. too
12. two

Review Words
13. sea
14. see

Adjectives with -*er* and -*est*

- Add -er to adjectives to compare **two** people, animals, places, or things.
- Add -est to compare **more than two** people, animals, places, or things.

Jan is tall.

Beth is <u>taller</u> than Jan.

Nina is the <u>tallest</u> friend of all.

Thinking Question
How many people, animals, places, or things are being compared?

 Write the correct word for each sentence.

1. Beth is _____ than Nina.

(quieter   quietest)

2. Jan is the _____ person of all.

(quieter   quietest)

3. Nina has _____ hair than Jan.

(shorter   shortest)

4. Jan has the _____ hair of all.

(longer   longest)

5. Jan has a _____ dog than Nina.

(smaller   smallest)

Focus Trait: Organization Details

A. Read each paragraph. Cross out the detail that does not support the main idea.

---

1. Gloria and Julian are different in some ways.

They both know how to fly a kite.

Gloria is a fast runner, but Julian runs slowly.

Gloria can turn a cartwheel, but Julian can't.

---

2. Gloria and Julian are alike in some ways.

Julian knows the best way to make wishes, and Gloria doesn't.

They like playing outside.

They go to the same school.

B. Read each main idea. Give a detail that supports the main idea.

Pair/Share Work with a partner to brainstorm possible details for each main idea.

Main Idea	Detail
3. Doctors and nurses are alike in many ways.	
4. Cats and dogs are alike in some ways.	

Lesson 22
PRACTICE BOOK

**Gloria Who Might Be
My Best Friend**
Phonics: Base Words and
Endings -er, -est

Base Words and Endings
-er, -est

Follow the direction for each question.

1. Who is **oldest**? Circle her.

2. Circle the **biggest** fish.

3. Circle the animal with the **lightest** color fur.

4. Who is **younger**? Circle him.

5. Circle the **taller** animal.

Write the correct word in the sentence.

6. longer   longest Anna's skirt is

_____ than Amy's skirt.

7. faster   fastest That is the

_____ car I have ever seen.

8. thinner   thinnest Eric is

_____ than his dad.

Understanding Characters

Read the selection below.

All of the kids were afraid of Casey. He always seemed grumpy. When he saw them, he would growl, "Get out of my way!"

One day, Casey found a dog without a collar. "Get out of my way!" Casey said. But the dog just wagged its tail and followed Casey home.

Casey went in his house and closed the door. He peeked out the window. The dog was still there. Casey opened the door. The dog jumped into his arms and licked his face!

"Hahaha!" Casey laughed. The kids in the neighborhood were shocked. They had never heard Casey laugh before.

"Come inside, dog," Casey said with a smile. "I'm glad you got in my way!"

Complete a Column Chart like the one here to tell about Casey. Then answer the questions about characters.

1. All of the kids were afraid of Casey. What does this help you understand about them?

_____

_____

2. What does the way Casey acts toward the dog help you understand about Casey?

_____

_____

Homophones

Circle the correct Spelling Word to complete each sentence.
Write the Spelling Word on the line.

Spelling Words
Basic Words
1. meet
2. meat
3. week
4. weak
5. mane
6. main
7. tail
8. tale
9. be
10. bee
11. too
12. two
Review Words
13. sea
14. see

1. A horse has a (mane, main). _____

2. Our town has one (mane, main) street. _____

3. I like to eat (meat, meet). _____

4. It is fun to (meat, meet) a new friend. _____

5. Seven days make a (week, weak). _____

6. A (week, weak) person is not strong. _____

7. I read a (tail, tale) about a cat with a long (tail, tale).

_____   _____

8. Who will (bee, be) afraid of a (bee, be)?

_____   _____

9. You can (sea, see) the (sea, see) at the beach.

_____   _____

10. (Too, Two) hippos are (too, two) big for the pond.

_____   _____

Lesson 22
PRACTICE BOOK

Using Adjectives

✏️ **Draw a line under the word in ( ) that correctly completes each sentence.**

1. Luis is (a, an) pal.

2. He goes on (a, an) airplane to visit George.

3. George cleans (a, an) attic upstairs.

4. Luis stays for (a, an) week.

5. The boys play in (an, the) park.

✏️ **Write the correct word for each sentence.**

6. The pond is _____ than the pool.
(deeper   deepest)

7. Luis is the _____ swimmer of all.
(faster   fastest)

8. Monday was _____ than Sunday.
(warmer   warmest)

9. January was the _____ month of the year.
(colder   coldest)

10. George is _____ than Luis.
(older   oldest)

Idioms

**Read each sentence. Choose the meaning from the
box that could replace the underlined words. Write the
meaning on the line.**

Meanings

stay cheerful   very special to him   understands what to do
does her best   tight and uncomfortable
---

1. Kim's grandpa is proud of her. She is <u>the apple of his eye</u>.

Very special tonim

2. Sally has been at her job for a long time, so she

<u>knows the ropes</u>.

tight and uncomfortable.

3. Jen had a good day at school. She always <u>puts her</u>

<u>best foot forward</u>.

stay cheerful,

4. Jay is sad, so Mel told him to <u>keep his chin up</u>.

understand what to do

5. I am so nervous! My stomach is <u>tied in knots</u>.

does her best.

88
10

Proofread for Spelling

Proofread the letter. Circle the misspelled words. Then write the correct spellings on the lines below.

Dear Jen,

    Our new house is nice. It is on Mane Street. We have too trees in the yard. I wanted to climb one, but Mom said it was two week.

    Lucky likes our new yard. He runs around and wags his tale. That silly dog bit at a be. I wonder if he thought it was meet to eat.

    This weak I start my new school. I hope I'll meat someone who wants to bee friends. I know we will have story time, and I think my new teacher is going to read a tail every day. Remember the story about the lion that lost his main?

    I miss you a lot. I hope you can come see me soon.

                    Your Friend,

                    Max

Spelling Words

Basic Words
1. meet
2. meat
3. week
4. weak
5. mane
6. main
7. tail
8. tale
9. be
10. bee
11. too
12. two

Review Words
13. sea
14. see

1. _____ 7. _____

2. _____ 8. _____

3. _____ 9. _____

4. _____ 10. _____

5. _____ 11. _____

6. _____ 12. _____

Subject-Verb Agreement

 Circle the correct verb to go with each subject.

1. She (play, plays) with me.

2. He (wish, wishes) for good luck.

3. We (throw, throws) a penny in the fountain.

4. They (hope, hopes) her wish comes true.

 Proofread the paragraph. Circle the four verbs with the wrong endings. Then write each sentence correctly on the lines below.

Julia is my best friend. She laugh at my jokes.

We watches a baseball game. She give me a sandwich.

We shares our toys, too.

1. _____

2. _____

3. _____

4. _____

Name _____ Date _____

Lesson 22
PRACTICE BOOK

**Gloria Who Might Be
My Best Friend**
Grammar: Connect to Writing

Ideas

My friend has a new dog.

His dog is <u>smaller</u> than my dog.

His dog is the <u>smallest</u> of all the dogs.

Rewrite the paragraph. Replace each underlined adjective with words from the box that compare.

the fastest of all	longer than my arm
stronger today than yesterday	the highest of all the kites

My friend Bob makes a kite. The tail is <u>long</u>. His kite looks like a bird. Bob takes the bird kite to the park. The wind is <u>strong</u>. Many people are flying their kites. The bird kite is <u>fast</u>. It flies <u>high</u>.

_____

_____

_____

_____

_____

_____

Suffixes *-y, -ly, -ful*

Circle the word that matches each picture. Write the word and underline the suffix.

1.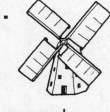
wonder (windy) *windy*

2.
(helpful) hopping *helpful*

3.
snoring (snowy) *snowy*

4.
(safely) softer *Softer*

5.
(careful) hurting *careful*

Have, Has, and Had

- *Have*, *has*, and *had* are **irregular verbs**.
- Use *have* and *has* to tell about present time.
- Use *had* to tell about something that happened in the past.

Subject	Present	Past
We	have	had
Glenda He, She, It	has	had
Ken and Marti They	have	had

Jean **has** a new rug now.

Dee and Ben **have** a red rug now.

We **had** a blue rug years ago.

Thinking Question
When does the action take place and who is doing it?

 Circle the word that correctly completes each sentence.

1. Carrie (have, has) two rugs.

2. Last week she (had, have) three rugs.

3. Now Gus and Lee (had, have) her old rug.

4. Carrie (had, have) no room for her rug.

5. Gus and Lee (has, had) room.

6. They (has, have) a big attic.

Suffixes *-y, -ly, -ful*

Choose a word from the box to complete each sentence.
Then read each sentence aloud with a partner.

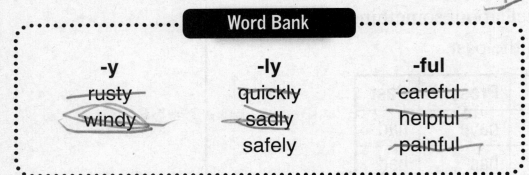

Word Bank		
-y	**-ly**	**-ful**
rusty	quickly	careful
windy	sadly	helpful
	safely	painful

1. Be _____carefull_____ when you
   cross the street.

2. _____Quikly_____ put the leash on Rover.

3. The old metal gate is all _____rusty_____.

4. The boy looked _____sadly_____ at
   his broken toy.

5. The splinter in my finger was _____Painful_____.

6. Put the money _____Quickiy_____ in
   your pocket.

7. Thank you for being so _____helpful_____.

8. It's so _____windy_____ that my hat
   blew away.

Conclusions

Waking up was hard for Max. His alarm clock couldn't wake him up. His mother couldn't wake him up. Max just kept on sleeping.

"Max!" his teacher moaned every morning. "You're late for school again!"

One day, Max came home and found his sister playing with a kitten.

The next morning, Max woke up with a jolt. Something furry was sticking its paw in Max's face! Max tried to go back to sleep, but the kitten kept pushing on his nose.

"Okay, okay," laughed Max. "I'm getting up!"

"Max!" his teacher cheered as Max walked into the classroom. "You're on time!"

"I know," grinned Max. Then he laughed again. "I have a new alarm clock!"

Read the story above. Complete an Inference Map to draw a conclusion about Max's feelings at the end of the story.

 waking up is hard to Max

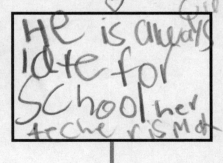 He is always late for school her techer is mad

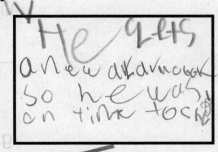 He gets a new alarm clock so he was on time to school

Conclusion: he feels happy because he was on time for school and his techer is happy

Suffixes *-ly, -ful*

Sort the Basic Words by the suffixes *-ly* and *-ful*.

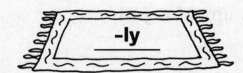

-ly

-ful

Spelling Words

**Basic
Words**
1. helpful
2. sadly
3. hopeful
4. thankful
5. slowly
6. wishful
7. kindly
8. useful
9. safely
10. painful
11. mouthful
12. weakly

Word + *ly*

1. Sadly
2. _____
3. _____
4. _____
5. _____

Word + *ful*

6. heiful
7. hopful
8. ta
9. _____
10. _____
11. _____
12. _____

Underline the suffix in each Basic Word.

Do, Does, and *Did*

- *Do*, *does*, and *did* are irregular verbs.
- Use *do* and *does* to tell about present time.
- Use *did* to tell about something that happened in the past.

Subject	Present	Past
We	do	did
Janet He, She, It	does	did
Pedro and Sam They	do	did

They **did** their best work with Jake.

He **does** square patterns.

We **do** striped patterns together.

Thinking Question
When does the action take place and who is doing it?

 Circle the correct word for each sentence.

1. Last week they (do, did) some patterns with Jake.

2. Jake (do, does) great patterns.

3. Yesterday, he (do, did) squares and triangles.

4. Now we (do, does) circles together.

5. He (do, does) his own pattern.

Focus Trait: Word Choice Synonyms

Writer's Words	Students' Own Words with Synonyms
You can <u>make</u> wool <u>beautiful</u> colors by <u>soaking</u> it in <u>dye</u>.	You can <u>turn</u> wool <u>pretty</u> colors by <u>dipping</u> it in <u>coloring</u>.

Read the words a writer wrote. Then rewrite the sentence in your own words, using synonyms.

Writer's Words	Your Own Words with Synonyms
1. You can <u>spin</u> wool into <u>threads</u> of yarn.	You can _____ wool into _____ of yarn.
2. A loom can be <u>built</u> using four <u>poles</u>.	A loom can be _____ using four _____.
3. You <u>start</u> weaving at the <u>bottom</u> of the loom.	You _____ weaving at the _____ of the loom.

Syllables *-tion, -ture*

Read the two words in each item below. Think about how the two words are alike. Then write the missing *-tion* or *-ture* word that fits with each pair of words.

Word Bank

-tion	**-ture**
lotion	creature
vacation	picture
fraction	capture
nation	nature

1. trip, travel, _____

2. animal, beast, _____

3. piece, part of, _____

4. grab, catch, _____

5. a drawing, a painting, a _____

6. weather, plants, _____

7. city, state, _____

8. sunblock, hand cream, _____

Name _____ Date _____

Lesson 23
PRACTICE BOOK

The Goat in the Rug
Deepen Comprehension:
Conclusions

Conclusions

Read the selection below.

My name is Missy, and I'm a golden retriever puppy. My owner, Molly, is filling up the bathtub. Why is she taking a bath in the middle of the day?

Oh! The bath is for me! Why is Molly giving me a bath?

Now we're in the car. I wonder where we're going. . . .

We just got out of the car. I see all kinds of dogs and lots of people, too. It looks like some people are studying the dogs. There's a table with big gold things on it. What are they?

Now Molly is leading me to a circle where other puppies are sitting. A man with a blue ribbon is looking at us and smiling. I wonder what will happen next.

Complete an Inference Map like the one here to draw a conclusion about where Missy and Molly are. Then answer the questions below.

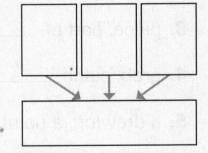

1. Where do you think Missy and Molly are?

   _____

   _____

2. Which details help you draw this conclusion?

   _____

   _____

   _____

   _____

Suffixes *-ly, -ful*

Write the Spelling Word that matches each meaning.

1. In a slow way _____

2. Wishing for something _____

3. Being weak _____

4. Having hope _____

5. In a sad way _____

6. Giving help _____

7. Being kind _____

8. Being put to use _____

9. In a way that won't hurt you _____

10. A lot of food in your mouth _____

11. Full of thanks _____

12. Full of pain _____

> **Spelling Words**
>
> **Basic Words**
> 1. helpful
> 2. sadly
> 3. hopeful
> 4. thankful
> 5. slowly
> 6. wishful
> 7. kindly
> 8. useful
> 9. safely
> 10. painful
> 11. mouthful
> 12. weakly

Irregular Verbs

  Circle the verb that correctly completes each sentence.

1. Last week the goat and lamb (have, had) long hair.

2. Yesterday they (have, had) a hair cut.

3. The lamb (has, have) short hair now.

4. The goat (has, have) short hair, too.

5. Now we (have, had) wool to make a rug.

  Write the correct verb to finish each sentence.

6. Gerry _____ something fun.
                    (do   does)

7. Tonya and Raj _____ a dance on the rug.
                    (do   does)

8. They _____ their favorite dance yesterday.
                    (do   did)

9. Gerry _____ his best when he jumped.
                    (did   do)

10. He _____ his best right now.
                    (do   does)

Name _____ Date _____

Lesson 23
PRACTICE BOOK

Multiple-Meaning Words

The Goat in the Rug
Vocabulary Strategies:
Multiple-Meaning Words

Read the words and their definitions. Decide which meaning fits each sentence below. Write the correct definition on the line.

foot	**1.** the body part at the end of the leg
	2. a measure of length equal to 12 inches
ruler	**1.** a person who is in charge of a country
	2. a long, flat object that helps you measure things
snap	**1.** to break
	2. to fasten or attach something
spin	**1.** to turn around quickly or twirl
	2. to make thread by twisting strands of fiber

1. That plant is one <u>foot</u> tall.

_____

2. The <u>ruler</u> of that country is very powerful.

_____

3. Don't pull the string too tight or it will <u>snap</u>.

_____

4. The weaver will <u>spin</u> the wool into yarn.

_____

Proofread for Spelling

The Goat in the Rug
Spelling: Suffixes *-ly, -ful*

**Proofread Bert's story. Circle the eight misspelled words.
Then write the correct spellings on the lines below.**

Last week we went to visit my grandparents' farm.
I couldn't wait, but my dad kept driving slowlee! When
we finally arrived, Grandpa took me to the barn.

In the corner of a pen, I saw a goat crying
weakely. Saddly, Grandpa said it was sick. The vet
gave Grandpa some pills. The goat ate them with a
mothful of corn. Grandpa was hopful that the goat
would get well. I stayed safly out of the pen. It would
be paynful if the goat kicked me.

Then I heard a tiny bark. I looked down to see
a wiggly puppy trying to climb onto my lap. Mom and
Dad let me keep him. I decided to call him Buster. I am
very tankful that we went to the farm.

Spelling Words

Basic Words
1. helpful
2. sadly
3. hopeful
4. thankful
5. slowly
6. wishful
7. kindly
8. useful
9. safely
10. painful
11. mouthful
12. weakly

1. _____   5. _____

2. _____   8. _____

3. _____   7. _____

4. _____   8. _____

Forms of the Verb *be*

✏️ **Circle the correct form of the verb *be*. Then rewrite the sentence on the line below.**

1. The women (are, is) weavers.

_____

2. The wool (is, were) soft.

_____

3. The rugs (were, was) pretty.

_____

4. We (are, is) interested in rugs.

_____

5. I (am, is) in a rug store.

_____

6. It (is, are) a new rug.

_____

7. That (are, is) the one I want.

_____

8. The other rugs (was, were) too large.

_____

Conventions

Wrong	Right
We <u>has</u> a new rug.	We <u>have</u> a new rug.

Read the paragraphs. Find six verb mistakes. Then rewrite each sentence. Make sure each verb matches the subject in the sentence.

Sue Makes Rugs

Sue have a loom now. She likes to weave rugs. We has a rug from her now. I watch Sue work. She do a lot to get ready.

Last week, Sue needed wool. Yesterday, Sue do a trade with the owner of the wool store. Now the owner have a rug, too. Now Sue have enough wool for many rugs!

_____

_____

_____

_____

_____

_____

Prefixes

**Make words with prefixes. Read the base word.
Then add the prefix at the top of the column and
write the new word.**

	un-	re-
1. lock	_____	_____
2. tie	_____	_____
3. pin	_____	_____
4. fold	_____	_____
5. pack	_____	_____

**Complete each sentence. Add a prefix from the box to the base
word at the end of the sentence. Write the new word on the line.**

over-	pre-	mis-

6. Set an alarm clock so you do not

_____. **sleep**

7. Before the real test, we will have a

_____. **test**

8. Be careful not to _____

any words. **spell**

Run, Ran and *Come, Came*

- *Run* and *come* are **irregular verbs**. You do not add an *-ed* ending to these verbs to tell about the past.
- *Run* tells about an action happening now. *Ran* tells about an action in the past.
- *Come* tells about an action happening now. *Came* tells about an action in the past.

Thinking Question
Is the action happening now or did it happen in the past?

Happening Now	Happened in the Past
The ducks **come** to the pond.	The ducks **came** to the pond.
The chipmunks **run** away.	The chipmunks **ran** away.

Read the word that tells when the action happens. Write each sentence using the correct verb.

1. The cows (come, came) from the fields.   **now**

_____

2. The children (run, ran) down the path.   **now**

_____

3. They (come, came) through the field.   **past**

_____

4. They all (run, ran) home before dark.   **past**

_____

Prefixes

**Read each word. Then write the prefix and base word
on the lines.**

1. unsafe _____ _____

2. recheck _____ _____

3. retell _____ _____

4. overeat _____ _____

5. unwise _____ _____

6. repaint _____ _____

**Add the prefix *re-, mis-,* or *pre-* to the base word at the end of
each sentence. Write the new word on the line to complete
the sentence.**

7. I _____ the oven before

   I bake. **heat**

8. I listen carefully so I won't

   _____. **understand**

9. I will study again and _____

   the test. **take**

Name _____ Date _____

Lesson 24
PRACTICE BOOK

Half-Chicken
Introduce Comprehension:
Cause and Effect

Cause and Effect

Read the following passage.

"My hat has a hole in it!" said Mandy. So Mandy and Mom went shopping.

Mandy tried on a dark pink hat. Pink was Mandy's favorite color. Mom did not buy the hat because it was too floppy. Mandy tried on a light pink hat with beads. Mom did not buy the hat because it cost too much. At last, Mandy tried on a bright pink hat with a yellow flower.

"It's perfect!" said Mandy. Mom bought the hat.

Fill in the T-Map to show the causes and effects.

Cause	Effect
Mandy's hat had a hole in it.	they oo so pint for a new has
the Dark pink hat was too flapy.	Mandy's mom did not buy the dark pink hat.
The light pink hat with beads was too expensive.	Mandy's mom is not goina to bay the right pix hat

Prefixes *re-* and *un-*

Sort the Basic Words by the prefixes *re-* and *un-*.
Underline the prefix in each word.

_____ re- _____   _____ un- _____

re- + word

1. retell

2. repaint

3. refill

4. remake.

5. read

6. replay.

un- + word

7. unhappy

8. untangel.

9. unkind

10. unlike

11. unpack

12. unlock

Spelling Words

Basic Words

1. unhappy
2. retell
3. untangle
4. unkind
5. repaint
6. refill
7. unlike
8. remake
9. unpack
10. reread
11. unlock
12. replay

See, Saw and Go, Went

- **See** and **go** are **irregular verbs**. Do not add an *-ed* ending to these verbs to tell about the past.
- **See** tells about an action happening now. **Saw** tells about an action in the past.
- **Go** tells about an action happening now. **Went** tells about an action in the past.

Thinking Question
Is the action happening now or did it happen in the past?

Happening Now	Happened in the Past
The squirrels **go** up a tree.	The squirrels **went** up a tree.
The squirrels **see** their food.	The squirrels **saw** their food.

Read the word that tells when the action happens. Write each sentence using the correct verb.

1. The chicks (see, saw) their mother.   **now**

the chicks see their mother

2. The chicks (go, went) with their mother.   **now**

the chicks go with their mother

3. All of the chickens (see, saw) the chicks.   **past**

All of the chickens saw the chicks

4. The chickens (go, went) quickly to their nests.   **past**

the chickens went quickly to their nests

Lesson 24
PRACTICE BOOK

Half-Chicken
Writing: Write to Inform

Focus Trait: Ideas
Exact Details

Sentence	Sentence with Exact Details
Animals live on this ranch.	**Horses, pigs, chickens, and cows** live on this ranch.

A. Read each sentence. Add exact details to make each sentence clearer and more interesting.

Sentence	Sentence with Exact Details
1. The hen ate.	The _____ hen _____
2. The chicks gathered around their mother.	The _____ chicks gathered around their mother _____ _____

B. Read each sentence. Look at the picture on pages 288–289 of *Half-Chicken*. Add exact details to make each sentence clearer.

Sentence	Sentence with Exact Details
3. Everyone came to see.	
4. Plants grew in the field.	

Silent Consonants

Write a word from the sentence to answer the question.

1. Would you **kneel** or **knit** a hat? _____

2. Would you **crumb** or **climb** a hill? _____

3. Would you drive **right** or **fright**? _____

4. Could you bend a **wrong** or a **wrist**? _____

5. Would you tie a **knot** or a **knife**? _____

6. Could a plane go **high** or **thigh**? _____

7. Would a **comb** or **lamb** eat grass? _____

8. Would you **wrench** or **wrap** a gift? _____

Use words from above to write two new sentences.

9. _____

10. _____

Cause and Effect

Read the following passage.

Two mice lived on a farm. One was named Meany. The other was named Silly. One day, the farmer's wife set some cheese on the table. Both mice wanted to eat it.

"I know how to get the cheese," said Meany. "I will scare the farmer's wife."

Meany made a mean face at the farmer's wife. She screamed and sent Meany away.

"I know a better way," said Silly. He ran into the kitchen and did a silly dance. The farmer's wife laughed and laughed. She gave Silly a big hunk of cheese.

Fill in the T-Map to show three causes and their effects.

Cause	Effect

Prefixes *re-* and *un-*

Write the Basic Word that matches each meaning.

Spelling Words

Basic Words
1. unhappy
2. retell
3. untangle
4. unkind
5. repaint
6. refill
7. unlike
8. remake
9. unpack
10. reread
11. unlock
12. replay

1. fill again _____

2. tell again _____

3. read again _____

4. play again _____

5. make again _____

6. paint again _____

7. not happy _____

8. not like _____

9. not kind _____

10. undo a lock _____

Irregular Action Verbs

Read the word that tells when the action happens.
Write each sentence using the correct verb.

1. The horses (run, ran) with their babies. **now**

the horses ran whith ther babies

2. The colts (come, came) to the water. **now**

the clts came to the whater

3. The animals (run, ran) for a drink. **past**

the animals ran for a drink

4. The boys (see, saw) the horses. **past**

the boys saw the horses

5. The girls (go, went) to the barn. **past**

the girls went to the barn.

6. The dogs (go, went) with the girls. **now**

the dog Go withthe girls.

Antonyms

Circle the two words that are antonyms in each sentence.

1. James put his wet shirt in the sun so it would get (dry).

2. Cindy put the (soft) pillow on the (hard) chair.

3. Nathan filled a tall glass with (water) and (sat) down to do his his short paper.

4. Amy used her strong arms to pull down the (weak) and (broken) branches of the tree.

Circle the two words in each group that are antonyms.

5. (swift)   (steady)   slow

6. (high)   (full)   empty

7. cold   (hot)   cloudy

8. (sunny)   hilly   (cloudy)

9. (before)   (over)   under

10. (smooth)   (bumpy)   brush

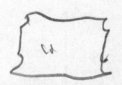

Proofread for Spelling

Proofread the newspaper article. Circle the eight
misspelled words. Then write the correct spellings
on the lines below.

Spelling Words

**Basic
Words**

1. unhappy
2. retell
3. untangle
4. unkind
5. repaint
6. refill
7. unlike
8. remake
9. unpack
10. reread
11. unlock
12. replay

New at the Ranch

The Wild Bill Ranch is getting a new prize bull,
Ollie.

This morning, ranch hands arrived to unpak a huge
crate. Out came a very unhapi bull.

"It might seem unkined to put Ollie in a crate,"
said the rancher. "But it was the best way to keep him
safe. Once we unlok the gate and untanglel Ollie from
his blanket, Ollie will soon forget about it. Ollie's new
space is unlik the small pen he once called home."

Watch the evening news to catch a repla of Ollie's
arrival. Or buy the book that reteels Ollie's story.

1. _____   5. _____

2. _____   6. _____

3. _____   7. _____

4. _____   8. _____

Commas in Dates and Places

Read each sentence. Rewrite each date or place. Put the comma in the correct place.

1. We visited Mexico on June 17 2009.

_____

2. I came from Atlanta Georgia.

_____

3. We saw horses on June 20 2009.

_____

4. Then I visited Chicago Illinois.

_____

5. The baby elephant was born on April, 2 2008.

_____

6. I heard about it in Avery Texas.

_____

7. I took a plane to Los Angeles California.

_____

8. I saw the chicks on May 1 2009.

_____

Word Choice: Using Exact Verbs

Without Exact Verb	With Exact Verb
The lions <u>move</u> quickly	The lions <u>dash</u> quickly.

Replace each underlined word with an exact word from the box. Write the new sentences.

~~race~~	hurt	~~watched~~	~~hid~~	squawks

1. Yesterday, I <u>saw</u> a fox.

Yesterday i watch afox.

2. I saw the fox <u>move</u> past our barn.

I saw the fox race past our barn

3. The chickens made many <u>noises</u>.

the chickens made meny squawks

4. Finally, they <u>sat</u> in their nests.

finally they hid in their nests

5. They thought the fox would <u>bother</u> them.

they thought the fox would hurt them

Words with *au, aw, al, o, a*

How Groundhog's Garden Grew
Phonics: Words with *au, aw, al, o, a*

Complete the puzzle with words that have the vowel
sound you hear in *saw*.

Read each clue. Then choose a word from the box.

Word Bank

toss	straw	tall	paw	salt
frost	pause	lost	soft	lawn

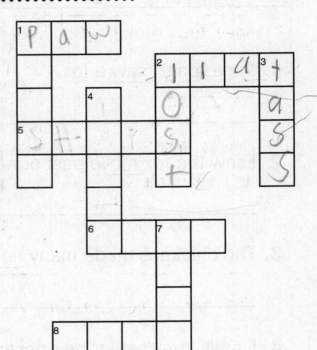

ACROSS

1. a dog's foot *paw*

2. cannot find *lost*

5. something to sip through

6. throw

8. gives food flavor

DOWN

1. a quick stop

2. grass

3. not short

4. icy coating

7. not hard

Say, Said and *Eat, Ate*

- The verbs *say* and *eat* are **irregular verbs**.
- *Say* tells about an action happening now.
  Said tells about an action in the past.
- *Eat* tells about an action happening now.
  Ate tells about an action in the past.

> **Thinking Question**
> *Is the action
> happening now
> or did it happen
> in the past?*

Happening Now	Happened in the Past
The groundhogs **say** they are hungry now.	Then the groundhogs **said** they were hungry.
Today, the groundhogs **eat** lunch.	The groundhogs **ate** lunch yesterday.

**Read each sentence. Underline the correct verb. Then
rewrite each sentence using the correct verb.**

1. Yesterday, the groundhogs (eat, ate) carrots.   **past**

_____

2. They (say, said) that they were still hungry.   **past**

_____

3. Today, they (eat, ate) tomatoes.   **now**

_____

4. Now the groundhogs (say, said) they are still hungry.   **now**

_____

Lesson 25
PRACTICE BOOK

**How Groundhog's
Garden Grew**

Phonics: Words with *au, aw,
al, o, a*

Words with *au, aw, al, o, a*

**In each row, circle the words that have the /aw/ sound
as in *saw*.**

1. flaw	hog	some	ball	soft

2. talk	cold	drawn	hang	launch

3. smoke	salt	small	faucet	off

4. toss	awful	cane	pale	water

5. mall	chalk	jaw	autumn	yawn

**Circle the word that completes the sentence and write
it on the line.**

6. Paul and I went for a _____.

    frost   walk

7. A _____ sat on a high branch.

    haul   hawk

8. I saw its sharp _____.

    claws   clogs

Name _____ Date _____

Lesson 25
PRACTICE BOOK

**How Groundhog's
Garden Grew**
Introduce Comprehension:
Sequence of Events

Sequence of Events

In 1995, chef Alice Waters decided to make a special garden. She called it the Edible Schoolyard. That's because she wanted schoolchildren to be able to eat the garden's food. Alice worked with students from a middle school in California to plant the garden.

The following spring, sixth graders started to work in the garden. In the fall, students helped to pick the vegetables. Seventh graders learned how to cook the vegetables in the garden's kitchen.

Every year, students planted more and different kinds of vegetables and fruits. They learned where food comes from and how healthy foods keep them strong.

Today, the Edible Schoolyard teaches students important lessons about nature, food, and healthful living.

Read the selection above. Then complete the Flow Chart to show the sequence of events in the selection.

```
┌─────────────────────────────────────────────┐
│                                             │
└─────────────────────────────────────────────┘
                      ↓
┌─────────────────────────────────────────────┐
│                                             │
└─────────────────────────────────────────────┘
                      ↓
┌─────────────────────────────────────────────┐
│                                             │
└─────────────────────────────────────────────┘
                      ↓
┌─────────────────────────────────────────────┐
│                                             │
└─────────────────────────────────────────────┘
```

Words with *aw*, *al*, *o*

Sort the Spelling Words by the /aw/ sound spelled *al*, *aw*, and *o.w*

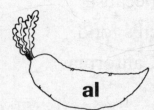

al

aw

o

al words	*aw* words	*o* words
1. tall	8. saw	12. dog
2. Call	9. draw	13.
3. fall	10. sawft	14.
4.	11. Paw	
5.		
6.		
7.		

Spelling Words

Basic Words
1. tall
2. saw
3. dog
4. draw
5. call
6. fall
7. soft
8. paw
9. ball
10. yawn
11. log
12. small

Review Words
13. all
14. walk

Give, Gave and *Take, Took*

- The verbs *give* and *take* are **irregular verbs**.
- *Give* tells about an action happening now.
  Gave tells about an action in the past.
- *Take* tells about an action happening now.
  Took tells about an action in the past.

Happening Now	Happened in the Past
They **give** the gardener seeds now.	Last fall they **gave** the gardener seeds.
They **take** the vegetables home now.	They **took** the vegetables home yesterday.

Thinking Question
Is the action happening now or did it happen in the past?

Read each sentence. Underline the correct verb. Then rewrite each sentence using the correct verb.

1. Last year, the children (give, gave) me seeds.   **past**

_____

2. I (take, took) the seeds to my garden last spring.   **past**

_____

3. All that summer, I (give, gave) the plants water.   **past**

_____

4. Now I (take, took) vegetables from my garden.   **now**

_____

Focus Trait: Voice
Using Your Own Words

Original Sentences	Writer's Own Words
Plants such as pumpkins, zucchini, yellow squash, and sunflowers grow very big. Their seeds need to be planted far apart to give them room to grow.	Some plants are very big. They need extra room to grow. Be careful not to plant their seeds close together.

Read each original sentence or set of sentences. Paraphrase each by using different words to give the same information.

Original Sentences	Your Own Words
1. Sometimes it is hard to find potatoes in a garden because they grow underground.	
2. Rabbits eat only plants. They use their long ears to listen for animals that might eat them.	
3. Bees and butterflies carry pollen from flower to flower.	
4. Some scientists believe the tomato first came from Mexico.	
5. Thousands of types of apples exist.	

Cumulative Review

Read each question. Make a word that answers each question by choosing a word from the box and adding the suffix *-y, -ly,* or *-ful* to it.

> **Word Bank**
>
> hand   rock   neat
> skill   bump

Which word describes . . .

1. a place with rocks? _____

2. someone with a skill? _____

3. working in a neat way? _____

4. amount held in a hand? _____

5. a road with bumps? _____

Add *-y, -ly,* or *-ful* to the word in bold print so that the sentence makes sense.

6. The kitten is very **play**. _____

7. She walks **soft** across the tile. _____

8. She gets **sleep** in the daytime. _____

Sequence of Events

Read the selection below.

Compost is a mix of rotting plants that makes dirt good for growing other plants. Good gardeners add compost to their dirt before they plant seeds.

Here's what you can do to make your own compost pile. First, pick a spot outside. Next, put scraps from your kitchen, like the peelings from vegetables and fruit, in your compost pile. You can add leaves and cut grass, too.

When the pile starts to grow, stir it up with a shovel. This gives it air. Air helps to turn the scraps into compost. Let a few days pass. Then sprinkle your compost pile with water.

After many months, you will have rich, black compost. Finally, take some compost and mix it into your garden's dirt. Your plants will thank you!

Answer the questions about the sequence of events.

Then complete a Flow Chart like the one shown here.

1. When should someone start to make a compost pile? _____

_____

2. Why will your plants thank you for mixing compost into the dirt? _____

_____

Words with *aw, al, o*

Write the Spelling Word that belongs in each group.

1. wood, tree, _____

2. foot, hoof, _____

3. cat, bird, _____

4. heard, touched, _____

5. paint, sketch, _____

6. bat, glove, _____

7. summer, winter, _____

8. shout, yell, _____

9. sleep, snore, _____

Spelling Words

**Basic
Words**
1. tall
2. saw
3. dog
4. draw
5. call
6. fall
7. soft
8. paw
9. ball
10. yawn
11. log
12. small

**Review
Words**
13. all
14. walk

**Write the Spelling Word that is the opposite of the
given word.**

10. hard _____   13. run _____

11. short _____   14. large _____

12. none _____

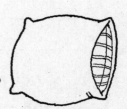

More Irregular Action Verbs

Read each sentence. Underline the correct verb.
Then rewrite each sentence using the correct verb that tells
about now or the past.

1. The farmers (say, said) they planted corn. **past**

The farmers said they planted corn.

2. Today, the children (eat, ate) a lot of corn. **now**

Today the children eat a lot of corn

3. The farmers (say, said) they can bring more corn. **now**

The farmers say they can bring more corn.

4. We (give, gave) vegetables to our friends. **past**

We gave vegetables to our friends.

5. They (give, gave) us fruit from their trees. **now**

They give us fruit from their trees.

6. We (take, took) two apples from the basket. **now**

We take two apples from the basket.

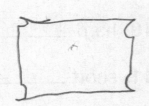

Using Context

Use clues in the sentence to find the meaning of the underlined word. Then find the word's meaning in the box. Write the definition on the line.

··········· Word Bank ···········

something that helps plants grow   move quickly
take small bites   speak with anger
someone who lives nearby   lucky

1. I like to <u>nibble</u> the carrot. I eat it like a bunny.

_____

2. Lisa is very late. She has to <u>rush</u> to catch the school

bus. _____

3. Please don't <u>scold</u> me. I did not mean to drop the

cup. _____

4. Jake is our <u>neighbor</u>. He walks to my house to play.

_____

5. Dad uses <u>fertilizer</u> in the garden. He wants the plants

to be healthy. _____

6. My sister has the flu. I feel very <u>fortunate</u> that I

didn't catch it. _____

Proofread for Spelling

How Groundhog's Garden Grew
Spelling: Words with *aw, al, o*

Proofread this journal entry. Circle the eight misspelled words. Then write the correct spellings on the lines below.

April 10, 2010

    I think spring is here. Today I sow a robin. I have not seen one since last fal. I like spring because I spend more time outside.

    I like to plant seeds in the sawft mud of Mom's flower garden. Then I drow pictures of the flowers on smoll cards and place the signs at the head of each row. My dog Max likes to help, but just one paw can smash my plants. Mom will call him away to chase his ball. Sometimes Max will just sit near me and yown in the sun.

    Soon my plants will grow toll. Then I will sit on a lawg and smell my flowers.

Spelling Words
Basic Words
1. tall
2. saw
3. dog
4. draw
5. call
6. fall
7. soft
8. paw
9. ball
10. yawn
11. log
12. small

1. _____ 5. _____

2. _____ 6. _____

3. _____ 7. _____

4. _____ 8. _____

Commas in a Series

Draw a line under each correct sentence.

1. Mom's garden has tomatoes, peppers and squash.

Mom's garden has tomatoes, peppers, and squash.

2. The squirrel, groundhog, and mouse eat the food.

The squirrel, groundhog, and mouse, eat the food.

3. The gardeners dig plant, and water.

The gardeners dig, plant, and water.

4. I planted the carrots celery and eggplant.

I planted the carrots, celery, and eggplant.

5. Mouse, Squirrel, and Rabbit watched the garden.

Mouse, Squirrel and, Rabbit, watched the garden.

6. They saw, bees, birds and butterflies.

They saw bees, birds, and butterflies.

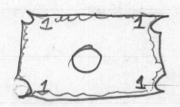

Name _____ Date _____

Sentence Fluency

Incorrect

Last week she **gives** me a bag of carrots.

I **taked** the carrots home.

Correct

Last week she **gave** me a bag of carrots.

I **took** the carrots home.

✏️ **Read this story about last summer. Write the paragraph correctly. Change each underlined verb to tell about the past.**

My Summer Garden

Last year, I grew a garden. I <u>take</u> seeds and put them in the ground. I <u>gived</u> them water. Mom and Dad <u>say</u> we could pick the vegetables when they grow. Soon, the garden grew. I <u>give</u> eggplant to Mom. I <u>take</u> carrots for myself. We <u>eat</u> it all. Yum!

_____

_____

_____

_____

Words with *oo, ew, ue, ou*

Put these letters together to write words with the vowel sound you hear in *zoo*.

1. m + oo + n __moon__

2. s + ou + p __soup__

3. c + h + ew __chew__

4. b + l + ue __blue__

5. p + oo + l __pool__

Now use the words you wrote above to complete the sentences below.

6. Did you see the __moon__ and the stars last night?

7. We swim in the __pool__.

8. I ate a bowl of hot __soup__.

9. The sun is shining in the __blue__ sky.

10. Our puppy likes to __chew__ on socks.

Contractions with *not*

- A **contraction** is a short way of writing two words.
- An **apostrophe (')** shows where letters were left out.

Whole Words	Contraction
do not	**don't**
does not	**doesn't**
is not	**isn't**
cannot	**can't**

Thinking Question
Which two words are being put together to make a contraction?

 Write contractions for the underlined words.

1. I <u>do not</u> believe my eyes! _____

2. Your pet <u>is not</u> friendly. _____

3. I <u>cannot</u> believe your pig can fly. _____

4. Your pig <u>does not</u> have wings. _____

5. I <u>do not</u> know how it can fly! _____

6. Our art teacher <u>does not</u> come on Tuesdays.

_____

Words with *oo, ew, ue, ou*

Answer each pair of clues using the words below the clues.

1. Something that helps solve a mystery _____

   The people who work on a ship _____

   crew   **clue**

2. To move quickly _____

   A place to see animals _____

   zoom   **zoo**

3. Many people together _____

   Got bigger _____

   group   **grew**

4. Lift or push someone from below _____

   In a little while _____

   soon   **boost**

5. Moved by using wings _____

   Not many _____

   flew   **few**

Story Structure

Max looked at the plant on his desk and sighed.
Why had his aunt given him a plant for his birthday?
It had a big purple flower and a strange-looking stem.

"Oh well," thought Max. He reread his favorite
book about the jungle, thought about going there someday,
and went to sleep.

He woke up in the middle of the night—and couldn't
believe his eyes! There were vines hanging over his bed!
There were big purple flowers everywhere! They all
reminded him of his new plant. . . .

Max played in his jungle until he fell asleep. When he
woke up, his room was back to normal. He looked at his
plant and smiled.

**Read the story above. Complete the Story Map to show the
characters, setting, and plot.**

Characters: max and max's plant	Setting: the Jungle
Beginning: he was looking at hi plant.	
Middle: he was dreming	
End: he was in reality.	

Words with *oo (ew, oo, ou)*

The Mysterious Tadpole
Spelling: Words with *oo*
(*ew, oo, ou*)

Sort the words by the spelling for the vowel sound in *moon*.

Spelling Words

With *oo*

1. root
2. spoon
3. bloom
4. room
5. boost
6. scoop
7. zoo
8. noon

With *ew*

9. crew
10. few
11. grew
12. stew
13. flew

With *ou*

14. you

Underline the letters in each word that make the vowel sound in *moon*.

Basic Words
1. root
2. crew
3. spoon
4. few
5. bloom
6. grew
7. room
8. you
9. stew
10. boost
11. scoop
12. flew

Review Words
13. zoo
14. noon

Contractions with Pronouns

- A **contraction** is a word made by putting two words together.
- An **apostrophe** replaces the letter or letters that were left out.
- Many contractions are made by joining a **pronoun** and a **verb.**

Whole Words	Contraction
I am	**I'm**
You will	**You'll**
She will	**She'll**
We are	**We're**
They are	**They're**
She is	**She's**
It is	**It's**

Thinking Question
Which two words are being put together to make a contraction?

 Write contractions for the underlined words.

1. <u>I am</u> surprised to see a pink tadpole. _____

2. <u>They are</u> supposed to be brown. _____

3. <u>It is</u> a funny looking creature. _____

4. <u>We are</u> not sure why it is so big. _____

5. <u>You will</u> wonder about this strange pet. _____

Focus Trait: Word Choice
Sense Words and Details

Without Sense Words and Details	With Sense Words and Details
Louis saw a tadpole.	Louis saw a **huge spotted** tadpole.

A. Complete each sentence, using sense words and details.
Use the hint in ( ) to help you.

Without Sense Words and Details	With Sense Words and Details
1. Louis touched Alphonse's skin. (touch)	Louis touched Alphonse's _BUPPY and lump_ skin.
2. Louis smelled the water. (smell)	Louis smelled the _STinKY._ water.

B. Read each weak sentence. Rewrite each sentence.
Add sense words and details.

Pair/Share Work with a partner to brainstorm powerful words.

Weak Language	Powerful Language
3. Alphonse ate a snack.	Airton treasure groove snark.
4. Louis heard a sound.	Louis heard a snicky sound downstars.

Cumulative Review

Add the suffix -y, -ly, or -ful to each word. Write the word on the line and read each completed sentence.

1. rain: I painted my bedroom one

_____rainy_____ day.

2. slow: I painted _____slowly_____.

3. care: I was _____careful_____ not to spill.

4. hope: Mom was _____hopeful_____ that I

would finish by noon.

5. quick: I tried painting _____quickly_____.

6. mess: It was _____messy_____.

Add the prefix to each base word. Then write the new word on the line.

7. re + paint = _____repaint_____

8. un + cover = _____

9. over + look = _____

10. pre + mix = _____

11. mis + match = _____

Name _____ Date _____

Lesson 26
PRACTICE BOOK

The Mysterious Tadpole
Deepen Comprehension:
Story Structure

Story Structure

Read the selection below. As you read, answer the questions to make predictions about what might happen next.

Jill named her new kitten Tiger because he looked like a tiger. Since Jill had moved to a new neighborhood, Tiger was Jill's only friend. She was scared of her new house.

One night, Jill heard a strange noise. "Oh no!" Jill cried. "What was that? I need to hide!" All of a sudden, Tiger came running in. As the little kitten ran, his body started to change.

1. What do you think is happening to Tiger? Why?

_____

_____

Tiger got bigger and bigger. He turned into a real tiger! The big cat stood up and guarded Jill's door all night.

In the morning, Tiger was a normal kitten. Jill patted his head. She wasn't scared anymore.

2. Why doesn't Jill feel scared now? Predict what might happen next.

_____

_____

Lesson 26
PRACTICE BOOK

The Mysterious Tadpole
Spelling: Words with *oo*
(ew, oo, ou)

Words with *oo (ew, oo, ou)*

Write the Spelling Word that matches each meaning.

1. not many _____

2. got bigger _____

3. animal park _____

4. raise _____

5. midday _____

6. pick up _____

Write the Basic Word that belongs in each group.

7. glided, floated, _____

8. team, helpers, _____

9. knife, fork, _____

10. chowder, chili, _____

11. kitchen, den, _____

12. flower, open, _____

13. tree, trunk, _____

14. me, us, _____

lling
ghton Mifflin Harcourt Publishing Company. All rights reserved.

Grade 2, Unit 6: What a Surprise!

Contractions

Write the contraction for each underlined word or words.

1. Tina knows that cats <u>do not</u> talk. _____

2. She <u>is not</u> sure why her cat can sing. _____

3. Tina <u>cannot</u> tell people about the cat. _____

4. She <u>does not</u> think anyone will believe her.

_____

Write each sentence. Write a contraction for the underlined words.

5. <u>We are</u> tadpoles in a pond.

_____

6. <u>They are</u> afraid of us.

_____

7. <u>You will</u> see that I am small.

_____

8. But <u>I am</u> going to be ten feet tall!

_____

Multiple-Meaning Words

Read the words and their definitions. Decide which meaning fits the underlined word in each sentence below. Write the correct definition on the line.

fly	**1.** a small insect with wings
	2. to move through the air like a bird or insect
line	**1.** a number of people or things in a row
	2. a long piece of string or wire used for fishing
upset	**1.** unhappy or disappointed about something
	2. to turn, tip, or knock something over

1. Ed used a worm as a hook on his fishing <u>line</u>.

_____

2. Sasha got <u>upset</u> when she heard the bad news.

_____

3. The kids waited in <u>line</u> to get a drink of water.

_____

4. An eagle can <u>fly</u> for many miles.

_____

5. The <u>fly</u> was buzzing around the picnic table.

_____

Proofread for Spelling

The Mysterious Tadpole
Spelling: Words with *oo*
(*ew, oo, ou*)

Proofread the paragraphs. Circle the eight misspelled words. Then write the correct spellings on the lines below.

Spelling Words
1. root
2. crew
3. spoon
4. few
5. bloom
6. grew
7. room
8. you
9. stew
10. boost
11. scoop
12. flew

Do yoo have a plant? When I groo up, I had a plant in my ruem. It was a pretty little tree. It grew inside a pot. Its rewts were deep.

I fed the plant every month. I gave it a fou scups of plant food. In the summer, I would bewst it up to the window so it could get more sun. Once a year, it grew beautiful red bloums.

1. _____   5. _____

2. _____   6. _____

3. _____   7. _____

4. _____   8. _____

Write these other Spelling Words in ABC order: *crew, spoon, stew, flew.*

9. _____   11. _____

10. _____   12. _____

Lesson 26
PRACTICE BOOK

The Mysterious Tadpole
Grammar: Spiral Review

Kinds of Adjectives

✏️ **Circle the adjective that best completes the sentence. Use the clue at the end of the sentence.**

1. The tadpoles are (big, brown). (color)

2. There are (forty, long) of them. (how many)

3. They are (tall, slippery). (feel)

4. They are (tiny, angry). (size)

✏️ **Read each pair of sentences. Join the sentences using and between the two adjectives. Write the new sentence.**

5. The ocean water was deep.

   The ocean water was cold.

   _____

6. The fish were happy.

   The fish were surprised.

   _____

Conventions

Incorrect	Correct
The mysterious horse <u>is'nt</u> growing.	The mysterious horse <u>isn't</u> growing.
<u>H'es</u> getting smaller!	<u>He's</u> getting smaller!

Read the paragraph. Circle five mistakes with contractions. Copy the story and write the contractions correctly.

The Mysterious Horse

Im' going to tell you a story. I once knew a pony named Lou. He was'nt a big pony. And he did'nt get any bigger, either. One day he started to shrink. H'es still getting smaller today. I think one day hel'l be the smallest horse in the world!

_____

_____

_____

_____

_____

Name _____ Date _____

Words with *oo* as in *book*

Word Bank

cookbook   ~~cook~~   ~~took~~
~~good~~   ~~cookies~~   ~~looking~~

Write a word from the box to complete each sentence. Then read each completed sentence.

1. My father and I like to ___cook___.

2. Last Saturday I was ___looking___ for something to do.

3. "Let's bake oatmeal ___cookies___," said Dad.

4. We followed all the steps in the ___cookbook___.

5. Mom ___took___ one of our treats.

6. She agreed that they tasted ___good___.

Write two rhyming words for each word below.

cook	good
BOOK	corstood
took	rood

Adverbs That Tell How

- An **adverb** describes a verb.

- **Adverbs** can tell about how something is done.

We lined up <u>quickly</u>.
We got off the bus <u>slowly</u>.

Thinking Questions
Which word tells how the action was done?

Read each sentence. Think about the action. Then underline the adverb that tells how the action was done.

1. The bus driver spoke <u>loudly</u>.

2. He <u>carefully</u> called each name.

3. She raised her hand <u>shyly</u>.

4. He <u>nicely</u> helped her climb the steps.

5. They got to the museum <u>quickly</u>.

6. <u>Quietly</u>, the children asked questions.

7. They looked at the dinosaurs <u>together</u>.

8. Then they talked <u>softly</u>.

Words with *oo* as in *book*

Name _____ Date _____

Word Bank

brook	hoof	hook	good	football
look	wood	foot	woof	cookies

Read the words below. Think about how the words in each group are alike. Then choose an *oo* word from the box that goes with each group. Write the word on the line.

1. hand, eye, ___book___

2. kickball, baseball, ___football___

3. nice, fine, _____

4. mane, tail, _____

5. moo, chirp, _____

6. creek, stream, _____

7. pies, cakes, _____

8. see, peek, _____

9. brick, glass, _____

10. bait, pole, _____

Name _____ Date _____

Lesson 27
PRACTICE BOOK

The Dog That Dug for
Dinosaurs

Introduce Comprehension:
Fact and Opinion

Fact and Opinion

Fossils are very old bits of bone, teeth, or
rock. Some examples of fossils are dinosaur bones, teeth,
and footprints that turned into rock. People study fossils to
learn about life millions of years ago. This is the best way to
understand the past.

Looking for fossils is hard. Scientists who study fossils
have to be very careful. They use special tools and spend a
long time digging each fossil out of the ground. They don't
want to harm any fossils. Scientists have found dinosaur bones
on every continent on Earth.

Everyone agrees that fossils are interesting.

**Read the selection above. Then list three facts and three
opinions in the T-Map below.**

Fact	Opinion

Words with *oo* as in *book*

Sort the Spelling Words by final consonants.

  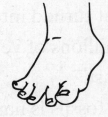

Final k	**Final d**	**Final t or f**
1. took	9. hood	13. foot
2. books	10. wood	14. hoof
3. cook	11. stool	
4. nook	12.	
5. shook		
6. crook		
7.		
8.		

Spelling Words

Basic Words

1. took
2. books
3. foot
4. hoof
5. cook
6. nook
7. hood
8. wood
9. stood
10. shook
11. crook
12. cookbook

Review Words

13. look
14. good

Adverbs That Tell When

The Dog That Dug for Dinosaurs
Grammar: What Is an Adverb?

- An **adverb** describes a verb.
- An **adverb** can tell about when something happens.

Yesterday, we went to the museum.

First, we took a bus there.

We wrote a thank-you letter today.

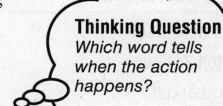

Thinking Question
Which word tells when the action happens?

✏ **Read each sentence. Think about the action. Then underline the adverb that tells when the action was done.**

1. Yesterday, we read about dinosaurs.

2. Today, we took a bus to the museum.

3. First, we got in line.

4. Then, we saw the fossils.

5. We will be writing a report soon.

6. Next, the children asked questions.

7. They looked at the dinosaurs later.

8. Then, they talked on the bus.

Name _____ Date _____

Focus Trait: Word Choice Using Adjectives

Without Adjectives	With Adjectives
I saw a dog.	**Look** I saw a <u>small</u> dog.
I felt his fur.	**Feel** I felt his <u>soft</u> fur.
He barked.	**Sound** He barked <u>loudly</u>.
I smelled something.	**Smell** I smelled something <u>fishy</u>.
I tasted a treat.	**Taste** I tasted a <u>sweet</u> treat.

A. Add an adjective to each sentence.

Without Adjectives	With Adjectives
1. Jake and his dog go for walks in the woods.	Jake and his dog go for _____ walks in the woods.
2. The woods have trees.	The woods have _____ trees.

B. Read each sentence. Rewrite it. Add adjectives.

Without Adjectives	With Adjectives
3. He feels the bark of trees.	
4. He smells the flowers.	

Lesson 27
PRACTICE BOOK

The Dog That Dug for
Dinosaurs
Phonics: Possessive Nouns

Possessive Nouns

Read the sentences. Draw a circle around each word that shows who or what owns something.

1. The bike's tire is flat.

2. We laughed at the seals' tricks.

3. The ladies' club has a meeting today.

4. The little rabbit's tail is white and fluffy.

5. The book's pages are torn.

6. The girls' team has a game on Thursday.

Now write each word you circled under the right heading.

One	More Than One
seals	tril
ladies	books
tire	rabbit

173

Fact and Opinion

Read the selection below.

Dinosaurs are more interesting than animals that live today. My favorite dinosaur is the triceratops (try SEHR uh tahps). It had three large horns on its head. It had a mouth like a bird's beak. It hatched from an egg. It looks friendly to me. I think that a triceratops would be a fun pet!

The smallest dinosaur was only the size of a chicken. It was fast and ran on two legs.

No one knows how dinosaurs sounded. I think that some of them probably sounded loud like lions.

Use a T-Map to answer the following questions.

1. Which details in the selection can be proven?

_____

_____

_____

2. What are some of the author's opinions?

_____

_____

_____

Words with *oo* as in *book*

Write the Basic Word that matches each clue.

1. Opposite of gave _____

2. To make food _____

3. Part of a coat that covers your head

_____

4. Things you read _____

5. A cow stands on this but you don't.

_____

6. A small place to sit _____

7. Got up from sitting _____

8. You put a shoe over this.

_____

9. A book used to make food

_____

10. It comes from trees. _____

11. A person who steals _____

12. Wiggled all over _____

Basic Words
1. took
2. books
3. foot
4. hoof
5. cook
6. nook
7. hood
8. wood
9. stood
10. shook
11. crook
12. cookbook

Adverbs

 Draw a line under the adverb that tells how or when.

1. Yesterday, we saw a show about dinosaurs.

2. We went there together.

3. We listened carefully to all the facts.

4. We took notes quietly.

5. Today, we are talking about the show.

6. Our teacher quickly lists the facts.

7. Tomorrow, we will write our papers.

8. Then, we will share our reports.

9. We will speak clearly.

10. The others will listen politely.

Synonyms

Choose the word in the box that has the same meaning as the underlined word or words. Write the word on the line.

Word Bank

huge   amazed   remove
messy   find   collect

1. Those dinosaur bones are <u>enormous</u>!

huge

2. The workers are going to <u>take away</u> the pile of dirt.

remove

3. We were <u>shocked</u> that a dinosaur could be so small!

amazed

4. Where do scientists <u>discover</u> fossils?

find

5. The scientist will <u>gather</u> the fossils she discovers.

collect

6. Please put those <u>dirty</u> tools in the shed.

messy

Name _____ Date _____

Lesson 27
PRACTICE BOOK

The Dog That Dug for Dinosaurs
Spelling: Words with *oo*
(*book*)

Proofread for Spelling

**Proofread the story. Circle the eight misspelled words.
Then write the correct spellings on the lines below.**

I had a funny dream. I dreamed I was sitting in
a nook next to an old fireplace. I could smell the wud
fire. Near the door, stud a huge cook. I knew because
he wore an apron and held a cookbuck.

He came over and shok my hand. Then he pulled
a hood over his head and started cooking breakfast.
It smelled gud. I saw that his right foat was not in a
shoe, but was a huf! He smiled at me. He looked like a
character from one of my story boaks!

1. _____		5. _____
2. _____		6. _____
3. _____		7. _____
4. _____		8. _____

Write these other Spelling Words in ABC order: *took, cook,
nook, hood, look, crook.*

9. _____		12. _____
10. _____		13. _____
11. _____		14. _____

Spelling Words

1. took
2. books
3. foot
4. hoof
5. cook
6. nook
7. hood
8. wood
9. stood
10. shook
11. crook
12. cookbook

Review Words

13. look
14. good

Using Adjectives

 Circle the word that correctly completes the sentence.

1. I found (a, an) fossil today.

2. It is the (bigger, biggest) fossil I have ever seen.

3. It may be (a, an) leg bone of a dinosaur.

4. The other bones I found were (shorter, shortest).

 Rewrite the paragraph. Add -_er_ or -_est_ to each underlined adjective. Write the new paragraph on the lines below.

I have the <u>great</u> dog in the world. His name is Chester. Chester digs in the park with his dog friends. Chester is <u>small</u> than his friend Chelsie, but he is the <u>fast</u> of all the dogs. He and his friend Luke find bones. The bone Chester finds is <u>long</u> than the others.

_____

_____

_____

_____

_____

Sentence Fluency

You can combine sentences that describe the same action. Use *and* to join the adverbs.

The tourists walked quickly. The tourists walked quietly.	The tourists walked quickly <u>and</u> quietly.
They are digging today. They are digging tomorrow.	They are digging today <u>and</u> tomorrow.

Read each pair of sentences. Use *and* to join the adverbs and write the new sentence.

1. We read about dinosaurs yesterday.
   We read about dinosaurs today.

   _____

2. I wrote my notes neatly.
   I wrote my notes carefully.

   _____

3. I'm going to study today.
   I'm going to study tomorrow.

   _____

4. I will answer the test questions slowly.
   I will answer the test questions correctly.

   _____

Words with *ow, ou*

Put these letters together to write words with *ow* and *ou*.
Then read each word aloud.

1. b + ow _____bow_____

2. c + l + ow + n _____clown_____

3. f + r + ow + n _____frown_____

4. l + ou + d _____loud_____

5. r + ou + n + d _____round_____

Now use the words you wrote above to complete the
sentences below.

6. Bubbles the _____clown_____ came out

on the stage.

7. He blew up a big _____round_____ balloon.

8. The balloon popped with a

_____loud_____ bang.

9. Bubbles had a big _____bow_____ on

his face.

10. Then Bubbles took a _____frown_____

while the crowd clapped.

Nouns Ending with 's

- A **possessive noun** shows that a person, animal, or thing owns something.
- When a noun names one person or thing, add an **apostrophe (')** and an **s** to that noun to show ownership. This makes the noun a possessive noun.

The <u>astronaut**'s**</u> ship is here.

Thinking Question
Who or what in the sentence owns something?

Read each sentence. Underline the sentence that shows ownership correctly.

1. Laura's mom is an astronaut.

Lauras mom is an astronaut.

2. Mom's room is filled with space gear.

Moms room is filled with space gear.

3. Dads workshop has pictures of planets.

Dad's workshop has pictures of planets.

4. The familys house is near the launch pad.

The family's house is near the launch pad.

5. My dogs favorite toy is a tennis ball.

My dog's favorite toy is a tennis ball.

Words with *ow, ou*

Word Bank

| couch | crowd | crown | found | frown |
| howl | mouth | ouch | round | shout |

Write a word from the box that matches each clue.

1. A part of your face _____ Mouth _____

2. A sound a dog might make _____ howl _____

3. A large group of people _____ crowd _____

4. A long seat for sitting _____ Couch _____

5. To yell loudly _____ Shout _____

6. Something a queen has _____ Crown _____

7. The shape of a ring _____ round _____

8. The face a grouch makes _____ Frown _____

9. What you say when you get hurt _____ Ouch _____

10. Got something you were looking for _____ found _____

Text and Graphic Features

Read the selection below. Use a Column Chart to name text and graphic features and tell why the author used each one.

The Sun, the Earth, and the Moon

Chapter 1: The Moon

The Moon is the easiest thing to see in the night sky. We see the Moon because light from the Sun reflects, or bounces, off of the Moon's surface and lets us see it.

Chapter 2: Changes in the Moon

The Moon seems to change shape from night to night. That's because the Moon circles the Earth. Each night we see a different part of the Moon lit up by the sunlight.

The Moon				
Day	Day 0	Day 7	Day 14	Day 22
Phase	new moon	half moon	full moon	half moon

Text or Graphic Feature	Purpose

Name _____ Date _____

Words with *ow, ou*

Sort the Spelling Words by the spellings *ow* and *ou*.

ow Words	*ou* Words
1. cow	7. house
2. town	8. shout
3. down	9. mouse
4. brown	10. found
5. flower	11. loud
6. now	12. around
	13. round
	14. out

Spelling Words

Basic Words
1. cow
2. house
3. town
4. shout
5. down
6. mouse
7. found
8. loud
9. brown
10. ground
11. pound
12. flower

Review Words
13. out
14. now

Write the Spelling Words that rhyme with each given word.

15. how, _cow_, _now_
16. blouse, _mouse_, _house_
17. clown, _brown_, _down_, _town_
18. bound, _found_, _shout_, _mouse_

Nouns Ending with s'

- A **possessive noun** shows that a person, animal, or thing owns or has something.
- When a noun names more than one and ends in **s,** add just an **apostrophe (')** after the **s** to show ownership.

The scientists' jobs are fun.

Thinking Question
Who or what in the sentence owns something?

Read each pair of sentences. Underline the sentence that shows ownership correctly.

1. The astronauts suits are hard to make.

   The astronauts' suits are hard to make.

2. The helmets' materials are strong.

   The helmets materials are strong.

3. The suits' materials are shiny.

   The suits materials are shiny.

4. Some scientists friends visit the lab.

   Some scientists' friends visit the lab.

5. The friends' smiles are bright.

   The friends smiles are bright.

6. The labs activities are exciting.

   The labs'. activities are exciting.

Focus Trait: Ideas
Details That Don't Belong

Opinion: It would be fun to ride in a space shuttle.

Details:

1. Gravity is different in space, so you can float.

2. You can eat astronaut food.

3. I once rode in an airplane to my aunt's house.

Detail 3 does not belong. It does not support the opinion.

Read each opinion and the details that follow. Cross out the detail that does not support the opinion.

1. **Opinion:** Everyone should exercise.
   Details: Playing sports keeps you healthy.
   Drinking water is good for you.
   Running can be fun.

2. **Opinion:** Working on a farm is hard.
   Details: In space, everything feels weightless.
   You have to do a lot of lifting and carrying.
   Farmers often work long hours.

3. **Opinion:** Being a veterinarian would be a great job.
   Details: You can be around animals all day.
   You get to make pets feel better.
   Some lizards can drop their tails.

4. **Opinion:** It can be good to try new things.
   Details: You might find something you like.
   You might realize you do not like something.
   Babies are very curious.

Cumulative Review

Fill in the blanks.

Word Bank

bloom
crew
toss
yawn
shook

1. It rhymes with **moss**.
   It begins like **took**. _____ *t oss* _____

2. It rhymes with **moo**.
   It begins like **cross**. _____ *crew* _____

3. It rhymes with **book**.
   It begins like **show**. _____ *shook* _____

4. It rhymes with **room**.
   It begins like **blue**. _____ *bloom* _____

5. It rhymes with **fawn**.
   It begins like **yes**. _____ *yown* _____

**Now use words you wrote above to complete the
sentences below.**

6. Many flowers _____ *bloom* _____ in the spring.

7. A good _____ *crew* _____ makes a ship
   run smoothly.

8. When it got late, Tony started to _____ *yawn* _____.

Text and Graphic Features

Read the selection below.

The *Apollo 11* Flight

The astronauts took off on July 16, 1969. It was the first time that humans had tried to land on the Moon. They called their flight *Apollo 11*. There were other flights to the Moon later.

More Flights to the Moon			
Name	**Launched**	**Landed**	**Returned**
Apollo 12	November 14, 1969	November 19, 1969	November 24, 1969
Apollo 13	April 11, 1970	did not land on Moon	April 17, 1970

Explain text and graphic features in a Column Chart.
Then answer these questions.

1. What type of graphic feature does the author use? _____

2. How does this graphic feature connect to the text?

_____

_____

3. Why do you think the author included this graphic feature? _____

_____

Words with *ow, ou*

Write the Spelling Word that matches each clue.

Spelling Words

Basic Words
1. cow
2. house
3. town
4. shout
5. down
6. mouse
7. found
8. loud
9. brown
10. ground
11. pound
12. flower

Review Words
13. out
14. now

1. You can watch it bloom in the spring.

_____

2. When you call loudly, you

_____.

3. A _____ is smaller

than a city.

4. The opposite of *lost* is _____.

5. You may live in one of these.

_____

6. A noise that hurts your ears is _____.

7. This tiny animal is afraid of cats. _____

8. The opposite of *in* is _____.

9. You get milk from a _____.

10. The opposite of *up* is _____.

Possessive Nouns

✎ **Underline the sentence that shows ownership correctly for nouns that name one.**

1. The ship's doors just closed.

The ships doors just closed.

2. The crowds cheers are loud.

The crowd's cheers are loud.

3. The boys ears are covered.

The boy's ears are covered.

4. The rocket's blast is starting.

The rockets blast is starting.

✎ **Underline the sentence that shows ownership correctly for nouns that name more than one.**

5. The astronauts' jobs are important.

The astronauts jobs are important.

6. All the rockets' engines must be checked.

All the rockets engines must be checked.

7. The mechanics work is hard.

The mechanics' work is hard.

8. The scientists measurements are correct.

The scientists' measurements are correct.

Classify and Categorize

Word Bank

crater	planet	sun	moon
float	comet	fly	orbit

Read each word above. Write each word in the best category.

How Things Move in Space	

Things in Our Solar System	

Proofread for Spelling

Proofread the sentences. Circle the misspelled word. Then write the word correctly on the line.

Spelling Words
1. cow
2. house
3. town
4. shout
5. down
6. mouse
7. found
8. loud
9. brown
10. ground
11. pound
12. flower

1. When you see your present, you'll showt with joy!

   ___shout___

2. Is that a stuffed mowse? ___mouse___

3. I have never seen a flouwer shop like that one!

   ___flower___

4. That restaurant has the best waffles in toun.

   ___town___

5. I have never seen her howse. ___house___

6. All of his clothes are broun. ___brown___

7. It takes a good caw to make good milk.

   ___cow___

8. Come on doun to the kitchen for dinner!

   ___down___

9. I fownd the book that I lost. ___found___

10. She dropped her sandwich on the grownd.

    ___around___

Irregular Verbs

 Circle the word that correctly completes the sentence.

1. The astronaut (have, has) a spacesuit.

2. For weeks she (does, did) many exercises.

3. She (has, have) a trainer who helps her.

4. Now she (did, does) jumping jacks every day.

 **Read the paragraph. Underline the six mistakes.
Then rewrite the paragraph. Make sure each verb matches
the subject in the sentence.**

Don have a great job in space. He do work on
the ship's engine. He have to take the engine apart
yesterday. He do his best to fix it. Now he have some
time to rest. He always do good work.

_____

_____

_____

_____

_____

Sentence Fluency

Weak	Strong
The boots belonging to the astronaut are new.	**The astronaut's boots** are new.
The job of the man is to fix the two-way radio.	**The man's job** is to fix the two-way radio.

Rewrite each sentence. Use a possessive noun in place of each underlined group of words. Write the new sentences on the line.

1. The brother of my friend wants to be an astronaut.

_____

2. The idea of my mom is to read a space book.

_____

3. The training of the astronauts is important.

_____

4. The hard work of a person will help her or him succeed.

_____

5. It is the dream of a boy to travel in space.

_____

Name _____ Date _____

Lesson 29
PRACTICE BOOK

Two of Everything
Phonics: Reading Longer Words:
Long Vowels *a* and *i*

Reading Longer Words: Long Vowels *a* and *i*

Write a word from the box to complete each sentence.

> **Word Bank**
>
> frightened   pasted   kindly
> racecar   higher   explained

1. The _____ woman likes to

   help at the neighborhood soup kitchen.

2. Dale's _____ was speeding

   around the track.

3. Dad _____ the problem in a

   way I could understand.

4. Were you _____ by the

   strange sounds in the middle of the night?

5. We watched the hot air balloon rise

   _____ in the sky.

6. Gina _____ the photos into

   her scrapbook.

Pronouns and Ownership

- A **possessive pronoun** shows that a person or animal owns or has something.
- *My*, *your*, *his*, and *her* come before a noun to show that someone has or owns something.

My <u>mom</u> gets two gifts.

Thinking Question
What noun goes with the pronoun?

Underline the possessive pronoun in each sentence.
Circle the noun that goes with it.

1. His presents are on the table.

2. Mom also sees gifts from her children.

3. Her daughter gives two books.

4. Her son gives two flowers.

5. Mom opens your gifts, too.

6. My mom has a good birthday.

7. Her sister called this morning.

8. My dad will take her out to dinner tomorrow.

Reading Longer Words: Long Vowels *a* and *i*

Answer each pair of clues using the words below the clues.

1. Doing something to have fun _____

   Water coming down from the sky _____

   raining   **playing**

2. Talk about things that trouble you _____

   Tell what something means _____

   explain   **complain**

3. Flashes of light during a storm _____

   Above something else _____

   lightning   **higher**

4. A track that trains run on _____

   A thing that plays music _____

   railway   **radio**

5. Bright and glowing _____

   Moving through the sky with wings _____

   flying   **shining**

Understanding Characters

Ella made clothes for the rich people in the town. Ella's only friends were the mice that lived in her cottage. She fed them and made them little coats.

One day, Ella saw a poster. The prince was having a party! "I wish I could go," said Ella. "Then I could meet people. But I have nothing to wear."

That night, the mice took extra pieces of cloth and sewed them together. They made a beautiful dress for Ella.

Ella saw the dress in the morning. "Thank you!" she said. "Now I can go to the party!"

Ella made lots of friends at the party. She wasn't lonely anymore.

Read the selection above. Then complete a Column Chart to better understand Ella.

Words	Actions	Thoughts

Name _____ Date _____

Words with *ai, ay, igh, y*

Sort the Spelling Words by the spelling patterns.

Long *a* Sound	Long *i* Sound
1. _____	10. _____
2. _____	11. _____
3. _____	12. _____
4. _____	13. _____
5. _____	14. _____
6. _____	
7. _____	
8. _____	
9. _____	

Underline the letters in each word that make the long *a* or long *i* sound.

Spelling Words
Basic Words
1. aim
2. snail
3. bay
4. braid
5. ray
6. always
7. gain
8. sly
9. chain
10. shy
11. bright
12. fright
Review Words
13. tray
14. try

More Pronouns and Ownership

- Some **possessive pronouns** stand alone. They are usually at the end of a sentence.
- *Mine*, *yours*, *his*, and *hers* are possessive pronouns.

Which <u>coins</u> are **yours**?

Thinking Question
Which word shows that someone has or owns something?

✏️ **Underline the possessive pronoun. Circle the noun that shows what is owned.**

1. The pennies are mine.

2. The dimes are hers.

3. The quarters are his.

4. The nickels are yours.

5. The money is mine.

6. Which bank is yours?

7. That wallet is his.

8. The purse is hers.

9. The dollar is mine.

10. The coins are yours.

Focus Trait: Ideas
Supporting Reasons

Good writers tell their opinions in responses to literature.
They give reasons for their opinions. They support their
reasons with examples from the story.

**Read the opinion. Then read each reason that supports
the opinion. Find an example from _Two of Everything_
that supports each reason.**

Opinion: The pot makes the Haktaks happy.

Reason	Example
1. The pot makes them rich.	
2. The pot helps them get a lot of things they did not have before.	
3. The pot makes them new friends.	
4. The pot helps them make other things they need.	

Name _____ Date _____

Lesson 29
PRACTICE BOOK

Two of Everything
Phonics: Vowel Diphthongs *oi, oy*

Words with *oi, oy*

Write the missing *oi* or *oy* word that will complete
each sentence.

> **Word Bank**
>
> joined   voice   cowboy
> noise   enjoyed   spoiled

1. The _____ sat by the campfire.

2. He had a very nice _____ for singing.

3. He _____ singing to pass the time.

4. Sometimes the cows _____ in.

5. Their mooing _____ his songs.

6. The lovely singing became frightful _____.

**Look at each word you wrote above. Match each one to the
word below that has the same vowel spelling. Write each
word below the word it matches.**

point   **toy**

_____   _____

_____   _____

_____   _____

Name _____ Date _____

Lesson 29
PRACTICE BOOK

Two of Everything
Deepen Comprehension:
Understanding Characters

Understanding Characters

Read the selection below.

Ant and Grasshopper were friends. They liked to sing, play the fiddle, and rest in the sun. When summer ended, Ant began to work very hard. He got wood and seeds and put them away for winter.

Grasshopper said, "Stop working, Ant. Come play with me." But Ant kept working.

Grasshopper shook his head. He wasn't worried. He rested and played.

Winter came. Ant was warm and cozy. He had wood for his fire and plenty of food. But Grasshopper was cold and hungry.

Finally, Ant said, "Come in. I'll share my food with you."

"Thank you, Ant!" said Grasshopper. "Next year I will work, too."

Complete a Column Chart to tell about the characters. Then make inferences to answer the questions about character traits.

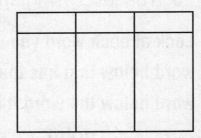

1. What can you infer about Ant's character traits and feelings? _____

_____

2. What can you infer about Grasshopper's character traits and feelings? _____

_____

Words with *ai, ay, igh, y*

Write the Spelling Word that means the same as the given word.

1. get _____

2. forever ___rright___

3. a scare _____

4. sneaky ___sly___

5. point ___aim___

6. shiny ___Bright___

Spelling Words

Basic Words

1. aim
2. snail
3. bay
4. braid
5. ray
6. always
7. gain
8. sly
9. chain
10. shy
11. bright
12. fright

Review Words

13. tray
14. try

Write the Spelling Word that belongs in each group.

7. plate, platter, _____

8. slug, worm, ___snail___

9. pigtail, ponytail, _____

10. quiet, timid, ___shy___

11. beam, light, _____

12. attempt, effort, _____

13. rope, leash, _____

14. sea, harbor, _____

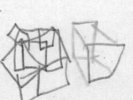

Possessive Pronouns

 Underline the possessive pronoun in each sentence.
Circle the noun that goes with it.

1. Dana and Dan are my pals.

2. The twins help you with your homework.

3. Her help is with math.

4. His help is with reading.

5. My friends like to help people.

Underline the possessive pronoun in each sentence.
Circle the noun that goes with it.

6. The skates are mine.

7. The hats are yours.

8. The bats are his.

9. The balls are hers.

10. The tickets are mine.

Name _____ Date _____

Lesson 29
PRACTICE BOOK

Two of Everything
Vocabulary Strategies:
Antonyms

Antonyms

Circle the antonyms in each sentence. Then write what each antonym means.

1. She put one purse into the pot and pulled out two.

_____

2. They worked late filling and emptying the pot.

_____

3. The branch swung high and low in the wind.

_____

4. The tiny mouse wanted to be as huge as a horse.

_____

5. The chair was heavy, but the pillows were light.

_____

6. Mike was glad to have a rest, but Patty was unhappy.

_____

7. Her dress was colorful, but her coat was faded.

_____

Proofread for Spelling

**Proofread the paragraph. Circle the six misspelled words.
Then write the correct spellings on the lines below.**

I am alwas late getting ready for school. My
mother says I am the only girl who actually does move
as slowly as a snayl. I take a long time to brade my
hair, and I brush my teeth over and over until they are
brite. Each day, I aym to move more quickly, but it
never quite works out. When I get to school, I have to
explain why I am late to my teacher. That is hard for me
because I am shi.

Spelling Words
Basic Words
1. aim
2. snail
3. bay
4. braid
5. ray
6. always
7. gain
8. sly
9. chain
10. shy
11. bright
12. fright

1. ___shy___   4. _____

2. ___aim___   5. _____

3. _____ 6. _____

Unscramble the letters to write a Spelling Word.

7. yar _____

8. lys _____

9. nachi _____

10. inag _____

11. bya _____

12. firght _____

Lesson 29
PRACTICE BOOK

Two of Everything
Grammar: Spiral Review

Irregular Verbs

 Write each sentence. Use the past tense of the verb.

1. Yesterday, dogs (run, ran) through the park.

_____

2. Two birds (come, came) after them.

_____

3. They (go, went) to the lake.

_____

4. They (see, saw) a giant rainbow.

_____

 Replace each underlined word with a word from the box. Write the new sentences.

came	went	saw	ran

5. The boys <u>watched</u> two movies.

_____

6. They <u>walked</u> to two games.

_____

7. They <u>dashed</u> around the field.

_____

8. Then they <u>traveled</u> to my house.

_____

Sentence Fluency

Weak	Strong
The teacher gave tests to the **teacher's** class.	The teacher gave tests to **her** class.
The student studied for the **student's** tests.	The student studied for **his** tests.

Rewrite each paragraph. Replace the underlined words with the possessive pronoun *mine, his, your,* or *hers.*

Miss Lee gave two tests today. Miss Lee got papers from <u>Miss Lee's</u> drawer.

Miss Lee said to the students, "Take out <u>the students'</u> pencils."

Dave took out <u>Dave's</u> green pencil. Annette picked up my blue pencil. I said, "That is <u>the one that belongs to me</u>.

_____

_____

_____

_____

_____

Reading Longer Words: Long *o* and *e*

Read the sentences. Draw a circle around each word that has the long *o* sound spelled *o, oa,* or *ow,* or the long *e* sound spelled *ee* or *ea.*

1. Rosa looked out the window on the coldest day of winter.

2. She noticed snowflakes floating down.

3. Slowly, the snow got deeper.

4. The snowplow went by on the street.

5. This might be the biggest snowstorm of the season.

Now write each word you circled under the word that has the same spelling for the same vowel sound.

folding	**blowing**	**freezing**
_____	_____	_____
_____	_____	_____
_____	_____	
	_____	
coasting	_____	**meaning**
_____		_____

Prepositions

- A **preposition** is a word that shows when, how, or where a noun or pronoun does something.

Chantel learned <u>about</u> Ben Franklin. She heard more <u>after</u> school.

Thinking Question
What word tells when, how, or where a noun or pronoun does something?

Choose a preposition from the box. Complete each sentence correctly.

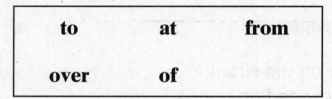

to	at	from
over	of	

1. My teacher chose a book _____ the shelf.

2. She turned to a chapter _____ the beginning.

3. Then she introduced us _____ the life of Ben Franklin.

4. We learned that he invented many things _____ two hundred years ago.

5. He also helped plan the government _____ the United States.

Name _____ Date _____

Lesson 30
PRACTICE BOOK

Now & Ben
Phonics: Reading Longer Words:
Long Vowels *o* and *e*

Reading Longer Words: Long Vowels *o* and *e*

Fill in the blank.

Word Bank

reason
steepest
sweeter
homerun
notepad

1. We hiked up the hill on the

_____ trail.

2. Tracey hit a _____ to win

the game.

3. Do you have a good _____

for being late?

4. Make a list of things we need on the

_____.

5. Cupcakes are _____ than popcorn.

**Read the words below. Think how the words in each group
are alike. Write the missing word that will fit in each group.**

Word Bank

loading
soapsuds
window
evening
leaving

6. morning, afternoon, _____

7. packing, filling, _____

8. door, wall, _____

9. moving away, going, _____

10. foam, bubbles, _____

Name _____ Date _____

Lesson 30
PRACTICE BOOK

Now & Ben
Introduce Comprehension:
Compare and Contrast

Compare and Contrast

George Washington's father loved him very much. When George was young, his father gave him an axe. George's father thought this gift would teach George about responsibility. George loved his axe. He chopped lots of bushes and branches on his family's farm.

There was one tree that George wasn't supposed to touch. It was his father's favorite cherry tree. One day, George made a mistake and chopped this special tree. This killed the tree.

George's father saw the dead tree and got angry. He called all the family together. George told everyone that he had killed the tree.

George's father was sad about his tree. But he didn't feel angry anymore. He was glad that George had learned to tell the truth.

Read the selection above. Complete the Venn diagram to compare and contrast the father's feelings before and after George told the truth.

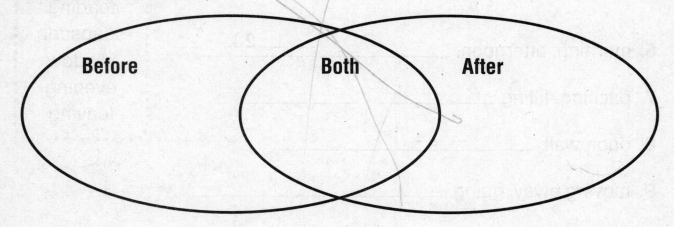

Before　　　　**Both**　　　　**After**

Words with *oa, ow, ee, ea*

Sort the Spelling Words by the long *e* and long *o* vowel sounds.

Spelling Words

Basic Words

1. seated
2. keeps
3. speed
4. seen
5. means
6. clean
7. groan
8. roast
9. bowls
10. crow
11. owe
12. grown

Review Words

13. green
14. snow

Long *e* Sound

1. seated
2. keeps
3. speed
4. seen
5. means
6. clean
7. green

Long *o* Sound

8. groan
9. roast
10. bowls
11. crow
12. owe
13. grown
14. snow

Now sort the words by how the vowel sound is spelled.

Long *e* Spelled

ee	ea
15. green	19. ____
16. keeps	20. ____
17. seen	21. ____
18. speed	

Long *o* Spelled

oa	ow
22. ____	24. ____
23. ____	25. ____
	26. ____
	27. ____
	28. ____

Prepositional Phrases

- A **preposition** shows when, how, or where a noun or pronoun does something.
- A group of words that begins with a preposition is a **prepositional phrase**. Many prepositional phrases tell where.

Ben Franklin runs **to the shop.**
He steps **inside the door.**

Thinking Question
Which group of words begins with a preposition that tells where?

✏️ **Choose a prepositional phrase from the box to finish each sentence. Write each sentence correctly.**

Prepositional Phrases That Tell Where	
near Ben's toes	in the mud
to the river	into the water
from his pocket	

1. Ben Franklin walks _____.

2. He steps _____.

3. Then Ben wades _____.

4. Tiny fish swim _____.

5. Ben takes a coin _____.

Focus Trait: Word Choice
Opinion Words and Phrases

Opinion	With Opinion Words
Ben Franklin was an important man.	**I think** Ben Franklin was **one of the most important** men in history.

Read each opinion. Add opinion words or phrases to make it stronger.

Opinion	With Opinion Words
1. Ben Franklin was the greatest inventor.	
2. Ben Franklin's hospital made his city better.	
3. The documents that Ben Franklin helped to write were very important.	
4. Ben Franklin's work in the past is important for our future.	

Final Stable Syllable -le

Read the clues. Then write one of the two words below each clue in the blank.

1. A kind of dog _____ beagle _____

A horn for making music _____ bugle _____

beagle   **bugle**

2. A sweet, crunchy fruit _____ apple _____

To eat in small bites _____ nibble _____

nibble   **apple**

3. Used for mending clothes _____ needle _____

A soft food in some soups _____ noodle _____

noodle   **needle**

4. Easy to do _____ simple _____

Peaceful or kind _____ gentle _____

gentle   **simple**

5. Burned to give light _____ candle _____

A small pool of rainwater _____ puddle _____

candle   **puddle**

Name _____ Date _____

Compare and Contrast

Read the selection below.

Do you do chores every day, like cleaning your room or walking the dog?

During the 1700s, children did many, many chores. Young boys hunted for food with their fathers. They also worked in the fields. When they were nine years old, they would start learning a special job, too, such as how to make horseshoes.

Young girls fed the chickens, picked berries in the woods, cooked food, washed laundry, and cleaned the house. They also cut wool off of sheep and spun the wool into thread. Young girls took care of younger children, too.

Children in the 1700s worked very hard.

Compare and contrast details from the selection with your own experience. Use a Venn diagram to help you. Then answer the questions below.

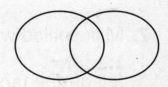

1. Think about the chores you do. What is the same about what you do and what children in the 1700s did? _____

_____

2. What is different about what you do and what these colonial children did? _____

_____

Words with *oa, ow, ee, ea*

Name _____ Date _____

Write the Basic Word that matches each clue.

1. in a chair _____

2. large black bird _____

3. how fast you move _____

4. to cook in an oven _____

5. not dirty _____

6. a croaking or unhappy sound

_____

Write the Basic Word that completes each sentence.

7. Milk spilled when the cereal _____

   fell off the table.

8. I _____ my brother 25 cents.

9. When I am _____, I will be much

   taller.

10. I have never _____ an eagle.

Spelling Words

Basic Words

1. seated
2. keeps
3. speed
4. seen
5. means
6. clean
7. groan
8. roast
9. bowls
10. crow
11. owe
12. grown

Review Words

13. green
14. snow

Prepositional Phrases

Complete each sentence by writing a prepositional phrase that tells when.

Prepositional Phrases That Tell When

before the sun came up   after he got in the water
after he ate breakfast   during the early morning hours
until that morning

---

1. Ben Franklin woke _____

_____ .

2. Ben went outside _____

_____ .

3. Ben swam _____

_____ .

4. Ben put on his flippers _____

_____ .

5. He had never used the flippers _____

_____ .

Dictionary Entry

Use the dictionary entries to answer each question.

> **e•lec•tric•i•ty** (ē′ lĕk·trĭs′ ĭ·tē) *n.* **1.** a form of energy that can be used for heating, lighting, or machines   **2.** an electric current
>
> **in•ven•tion** (in·vĕn′ shən) *n.* **1.** something that is created or made for the first time   **2.** a story that is made up
>
> **light•ning** (līt′ nĭng) *n.* **1.** a flash of light in the sky caused by an electrical charge in the clouds
>
> **wig** (wĭg) *n.* **1.** fake hair that is worn on the head

1. How many syllables does the word *electricity* have?

_____

2. What part of speech is the word *wig*? _____

3. How many syllables does the word *invention* have?

_____

4. How many definitions does the word *lightning* have?

_____

Choose one word from the dictionary entries. Write a sentence with the word.

5. _____

Proofread for Spelling

**Proofread the postcard. Circle the six misspelled words.
Then write the correct spellings on the lines below.**

Dear Tomas,

    You would not believe the things we have
sean on our trip. We went to a place where potters make
clay boals big enough to sit in! Can you imagine being
seeted in a pot? Each pattern meens something different.
If a crowe is painted, it is for good luck. I hope the town
keaps making the pottery so you can see it someday.

               Manny

Spelling Words

Basic Words
1. seated
2. keeps
3. speed
4. seen
5. means
6. clean
7. groan
8. roast
9. bowls
10. crow
11. owe
12. grown

Review Words
13. green
14. snow

1. _____ 4. _____

2. _____ 5. _____

3. _____ 6. _____

Unscramble the letters to write a Spelling Word.

7. angro _____

8. weo _____

9. despe _____

10. leanc _____

11. stoar _____

12. rowng _____

Irregular Verbs

✏️ **Underline the correct verb to finish each sentence. Use the clue that tells when the action happens.**

1. We (give, gave) reports today. **Now**

2. I (take, took) the topic of Ben Franklin. **Past**

3. Sara and I (eat, ate) lunch. **Past**

4. The teacher (say, said) I could give my report first. **Past**

✏️ **Read this story about something that happened last week. Write the underlined words correctly. Use verbs that tell about the past.**

I <u>eat</u> lunch with my sister. She <u>give</u> me a library book. It was about Ben Franklin. She <u>say</u> she liked it. I <u>take</u> the book to my room. It was a good book. Ben Franklin <u>give</u> the world many things. It <u>take</u> me just a little while to read the book.

_____

_____

_____

_____

Sentence Fluency

Two Sentences	Combined Sentence
Sam read about Ben Franklin. Ann read about Ben Franklin.	Sam and Ann read about Ben Franklin.

 Read each pair of sentences. Combine the sentences.
Use *and* to join their subjects.

1. Jessie learned about electricity.

Maria learned about electricity.

_____

2. Our teacher talked about freedom.

The principal talked about freedom.

_____

3. Susan liked hearing about inventors.

Jamie liked hearing about inventors.

_____

4. Mike enjoyed reading about Ben Franklin.

The other children enjoyed reading about Ben Franklin.

_____

_____

the end